24.95 Mumford

Personal Success

Success

Bottom AND THE Line

Mark C. Middleton

SUCCESS PUBLISHING, INC.

SUCCESS PUBLISHING, INC.
P.O. Box 1341
Elfers, FL 34680-1341

Permissions
Mark C. Middleton
C/O Success Publishing, Inc.
P.O. Box 1341
Elfers, FL 34680-1341

Cover Design: George Foster – Foster & Foster, Inc.

Printed in the United States by Vaughan Printing – Nashville, TN

Library of Congress Catalog Card Number TXu1-254-489

ISBN 0-9772801-0-1

Visit my website at **www.marksaid.com**

Disclaimer

The material gathered prior to the initial writing of this book was assembled from personal knowledge, training, observations and experiences. After initial substantial completion, additional extensive reading and research was done in order to substantiate and provide authoritative references. This involved the reading, review and study from a great number of sources.

In all cases, whenever supportive material is used or referenced, all attempts have been made to acknowledge proper credit to that source. However, it is certainly possible that there exists a similarity in my own established stated positions and conclusions that might closely parallel those of others whether reviewed by me or not.

If any credits are found to be incomplete, inaccurate or not properly identified, I apologize. Any error is not intentional and is exactly that, an error.

My sole intent is to help you understand and recognize how and why others have succeeded and be better prepared to control your own future and, hopefully, maybe even enjoy the process.

The information contained herein is not intended to replace any professional advice and is being provided for use at the discretion of the reader. No representations are made by either the author or the publisher as to any results or individual degree of accomplishment by the application of any concepts, procedures, recommendations or suggestions contained herein.

Introduction

Success is a mix of doing the right things well and not doing the wrong things at all (or at least less often).

As an accountant, I have spent over twenty-five years helping my clients make decisions ranging from personnel staffing, to capital expenditures, to paying for Jenny to attend Princeton. In business and in life, there aren't many decisions that don't involve money, therefore I seem to be involved in a wide array of matters that you typically wouldn't think requires the advice of a finance geek.

This is not to say money is THE most important thing, just that it is a necessity of our culture. I used to think that there were typically two outlooks on financial success. The first is that money is a scorecard, and the one with the most toys wins. The second is that money is no more than a means to an end. I have had the unusual advantage of being a follower of both beliefs. As a result of a serious automobile accident in 1993, I was touch and go with death and lucky enough to come away with my life. As anyone who has had such an experience can attest to, these things have a way of realigning your priorities (bad news was that my spine was permanently realigned and held together with screws). In an instant I knew that "money as a scorecard" was not important and that success was not just defined by who had the most money.

This also affected how I did business. Similar to the money philosophy, there are two analogous business philosophies. The first is the ideology of working for a commission or paycheck, and caring for the customer as a means to that end. The second is working for the customer with or without the financial motivation. In reality we all probably find ourselves somewhere in between on this spectrum. However, it has been my experience that the people who fall into the latter category are happier.

Following my accident my outlook shifted significantly to really wanting to help my clients achieve their individual success. I had always helped them achieve financial success, but now my focus was to understand how they defined success individually. Was it the sense of achievement in creating a business that provides some societal good? Maybe it is having the time to be with friends and family. For some it is a search for knowledge in some form, and for others it really was about wealth creation and status. Understanding how people define success helps me be a better advisor.

This understanding empowered me to go beyond the traditional role of an accountant to become a mentor. It also opened my eyes as to the character traits and actions of my clients. I started seeing patterns in one group of people who seemed to have the ability to achieve their own definition of success, and others that seemed to be always treading water – either because they were not able to reach their goals or because they were shooting for the wrong goals. As a naturally inquisitive person, I set out to determine the commonalities among the successful and the flaws common among the water treaders. In conjunction with that, I became a student on the study of success and read everything I could get my hands on about the subject.

My goal is to pass on what I have learned from both this empirical study and book research. I want to help you learn the skills and traits you need to be successful. As importantly, I want to help you avoid many of the mistakes that the "water treading" group makes.

The many true-life examples and stories that you will read are designed to provide you with a lifetime of experience to complement the more academic study of how to be successful. You will take with you succinct skills that will have a measurable impact on all aspects of your life and aid in your journey towards achieving

PERSONAL SUCCESS

Contents

Preparing Your Mind for Success

CHAPTER ONE

An Open Mind

"It is better to know nothing than to know what ain't so."
— Josh Billings

WEBSTER'S
"Receptive to new ideas or to reason."

MINE
*"Not predisposed to advance preconceptions,
impressions, stereotypes or judgments."*

Prior to meeting someone do you at least begin to develop an impression of them based upon their profession, name, age, sex, religion, picture, ethnicity, something that you know or find out in advance? Sure you do. We all will.

I had the occasion to have a conversation about this with a successful businessman that I had a long business and personal relationship with. I think this individual provided the best lesson on how to approach a meeting, business proposal, social event, meeting someone or interview with an open mind. Not just keeping an open mind, but also and more importantly having an open mind to begin with.

He tried to clear his mind of any preconceived opinions or judgments from the start. He wanted to avoid focusing and being influenced only on the facts that might support any preconceptions prior to the presentation of all the information and, therefore, cloud his judgment in making the best overall decision, and permitting the situation or other person to have a fair chance.

According to Jack Deal of Deal Consulting, in his work he has found that "Open minds take more risks ... also succeed more often and have a greater degree of success." In his work he has found that closed minded people usually seek out others who are also closed minded, less intelligent and less capable.

As Karim Hajee, founder of the *Creating Power System*, states, *"When you have an open mind you allow yourself to attract opportunities ... When you close your mind ... you end up having an attitude ... (that) shuts you off from the process of life and nature – which is about growing and experiencing new possibilities."*

Having a closed mind is the result of habitually filtering out, ignoring, rejecting and discounting information, facts and ideas that don't fit your preconceptions or prior decisions. Or, maybe it results from simply not listening at all. By doing so, you can miss great opportunities for developing personal relationships, allies, business opportunities, investments or simply learning and growing as a person.

Seeing a picture before meeting a lady, the employee comments, "She has mean eyes." You could tell by her voice inflection and body language that when the other person arrived she was looking only for those characteristics that would support her advance opinion based upon the picture.

Carol the new office manager was to start at a salon the next day. An employee, Mary, having met Carol for only a few minutes the day before tells the other employees that Carol is a hyper bossy person. All the employees then decided that they didn't like her even before they met her. Carol ended up quitting within three weeks.

Prior to entering a meeting with Robin, a well educated professional manager, Jeff, an older lesser educated associate gruffly states, "There is nothing this young punk has to say that I am interest in." Sure enough, after the meeting Jeff declares, "That was a waste of time." It wasn't that there was nothing he could learn from Robin, it was that Jeff had already decided prior to the meeting that there was nothing he was going to learn.

Is it possible that each of us individually does not have all the answers? Kim Krisco author of Leadership and the Art of Conversation: Conversation as a Management Tool and other books established "Krisco's Humble Pie". This estimates that, at any given time on any given subject:

What we know	25%
What we know we don't know	25%
What we don't know we don't know	50%

Have any of the following situations ever happened to you?

Told yourself that you weren't going to like a movie before seeing it based upon the title or who's in it, what it's about, the subject?

Concluded that you were not going to like some outing before even going? An example might be a trip to the mall, beach, park, restaurant, etc.

Decided that you were not going to enjoy some social activity? An example might be a family gathering, party, holiday or social event, etc.

I am willing to bet that in almost all of those cases, you were right. You did not enjoy it. Not necessarily because it wasn't enjoyable, but rather because you had already decided that you were not going to have any fun. You were doomed from the beginning.

Have any of the following ever happened to you?

Purchased or been given an electronic item (television, computer, printer, VCR or DVD players) telling yourself that you probably won't be able to figure out how to hook it up, use or program it?

Begin a home project like painting, laying tile, installing light fixtures, building shelves, and either before beginning the project or shortly into it make up your mind that it isn't going to come out right?

Wanted a job but before applying somewhere said something like, "They are not going to hire me."?

Been in a classroom or position where someone is trying to teach you something but you are telling yourself that you can't do this?

Again, I will bet that in most of those cases you were right and whatever you told yourself was or was not going to happen before you even tried, did.

Borrowing a lesson from a movie line: *"You should never begin a relationship (or project) trying to live up to such low expectations."*

Some guidelines for keeping an open mind:

Humility – Know that it is possible, just possible that you don't already have all the answers.

Don't know – Accept that not only is there much you don't know, there is much that you don't know that you don't know.

Curiosity – Curiosity recognizes that no two people see things exactly the same. Be curious about others perspectives and opinions, and less adamant about the validity of your own.

Want to learn – Begin with the desire and intent to learn.

Approach with a new attitude – "In the beginner's mind there are many possibilities, but in the expert's there are few."

Be receptive to new ideas – Don't automatically take a contrarian position to others ideas, especially before you hear them.

Practice equality – Treat everyone as equals.

Truthfulness with tact – Be truthful but without blame, judgment or condescension.

Respect – Always extend respect to and for others and for yourself.

Some enemies of an open mind:

Doubt – We all have had life experiences. Doubt is a self defense mechanism that prevents us from being taken advantage of, trusting in our own judgment over others.

Stubborn – Nobody likes to admit that they are wrong and some people can't admit it no matter what evidence there is against them.

Gone to far – Some people have spent years believing some thing that maybe wasn't right to begin with or simply isn't right any longer. They can't accept that they were wrong all that time. Taking the right road can only occur if you get off the wrong road.

―――◦◦◦――――

"The ancient Master didn't try to educate the people,
but kindly taught them to not-know answers.
When they think they know the answers,
People are difficult to guide.
When they know that they don't know,
People can find their own way ..."

— From the *Tao Te Ching*

AN OPEN MIND

1. *Have an open mind.* Don't enter a relationship, meeting, social event, project or outing with preconceived conclusions.
2. *If you have already made up your mind* beforehand, you will most certainly almost always be right, unfortunately.
3. *Humility* will accept that you may not already have all the answers. It is just possible that someone else might have some of them.
4. *Be curious* – Want to learn.
5. *Be receptive* to new or different ideas.
6. Respect others and yourself. Treat all as equals and be truthful.
7. *Stubbornness* is a weakness that keeps you on the wrong road.

AND MOST IMPORTANTLY

8. *Have an open mind while reading this book.* Many successful people have contributed their knowledge and experience for your benefit.

THE BOTTOM LINE

When you make up your mind before even trying, then you aren't trying. Entering a relationship or project with an open mind doesn't mean that you don't give it some thought before entering, that's just being prepared. Receiving and processing all of the information and facts is learning. Letting the information and facts make your decision is education. Having a closed mind is ignorance.

Q. What movie is the following line from?

"Mind like parachute – only function when open."

CHAPTER TWO

The Big Picture and the Small Stuff

"See what no one else sees. See what everyone chooses not to see ... out of fear, conformity or laziness. See the whole world anew each day"

— Patch Adams

WEBSTER'S
"A long range or overall view or account of some complex matter."

MINE
"The continued pursuit of the future or whole rather than the distraction of the moment or part."

**The Big Picture is what is important.
Everything else doesn't matter. It is the small stuff.**

"Can't see the forest for the trees."

"Penny wise and pound foolish."

"We won the battle but lost the war."

"Is the bang worth the buck?"

"Don't spit into the wind." (Okay, probably not on point,
but just seeing if you're paying attention).

It is easy to be distracted from or lose track of The Big Picture. Caught up in the moment, living for the day, following your emotions. Thinking with your, *insert your own here*, and not your brain. To be successful, you must stay focused on and not get distracted from your ultimate goal(s).

---

*"You can't depend on your judgment
when your imagination is out of focus."*

— Mark Twain

John and Frank, the owners of an Electrical Contracting Company set out to become the largest in the County. They aggressively marketed their services to builders, residential and commercial. After a year and much funding from John and Frank, the Company had several major contracts, a large office facility and many employees, but the Company continued to need cash invested by the owners. After an update and analysis of accurate financial statements, I met with John and Frank and explained that their direct labor, materials and direct variable overhead costs were 102% of contracts before deducting fixed office overhead. They were so focused on getting contracts and becoming the biggest they had lost sight of profitability.

"Can't see the forest for the trees." I remember talking with a young man the day of his wedding. At that time he drove an old car, had a

crummy job, shared an apartment and had no savings or direction in life. I asked him what he wanted out of life. He said that all he wanted was a loving and caring wife as his partner, and be able to afford their own home and start a family.

After several years, he is still married; they purchase a nice home and have two healthy children. His business is not doing as well as he would like and his negative emotions in dealing with this could jeopardize their marriage. He already has achieved his original Big Picture but is risking losing it by only focusing on the small stuff.

I believe he had lost sight of his Big Picture. (Keep this in mind later during the chapter *Recognizing Success).*

Consider, as an example, a wedding reception ending with a fight between guests or family members resulting usually from to much alcohol consumption. Parents, siblings, in-laws that may not approve of the new spouse, whatever the cause. Sometimes even ends with arrests. Those individuals certainly lost sight of The Big Picture, participating in the celebration of a marriage.

Consider a common every day activity performed by most of us, to drive somewhere: school, the mall, work, movies, sports events, etc. The Big Picture is to get from one point to another, safely. To lose sight of The Big Picture is to be so distracted by something or someone else that you fail to get to your destination and back, safely.

To lose sight of The Big Picture and get distracted by the small stuff is to put yourself and others at risk when getting drawn into something you shouldn't by the jerk that cuts you off in traffic or runs the red traffic signal causing you to slam on your brakes. Staying focused on The Big Picture would be to ignore them and complete your journey safely.

According to a study by the AAA Foundation for Traffic Safety, about 25% of all traffic accidents are a result of distractions. The following ranked as the most common driving distractions that we all individually may engage in:

Reaching, leaning for something	97%
Using radio controls	91%
Involved in conversation	77%
Eating, drinking	71%
Personal grooming	45%
Distracted by passenger(s)	44%
Reading or writing	40%
Using cell phone	30%
Smoking	7%

If you are involved in a traffic accident resulting from one of the reasons above, then you probably lost sight of The Big Picture.

Usually The Big Picture doesn't change, although details and specifics might. Take for example the high school graduate whose big picture is to attend college followed by employment in their chosen field. Applying at a prestigious University, fails to be accepted, however, is accepted at another fine College or University. Their Big Picture remains intact, simply one detail or specific changed.

Another consideration, it has been well established that your point of beginning is less important than how you apply and use what you learn along the way. Meaning, graduating from Harvard provides an advantage but it is less important than life experiences and applying what you have learned from those life experiences. Therefore, at any given time or point in your life, building on your prior life experiences is more valuable than your point of beginning of formal education or wealth in preparing for and shaping your future, achieving your goals and having The Big Picture.

Knowledge is Power.

Education is Power.

Information is Power.

Training is Power.

Ability is Power.

Action is Power.

Experience is Powerful!

This is worth repeating – **Your point of beginning is less important than what you learn and apply during your journey.**

"But I never went to college."

"I don't have any money."

"My parents didn't help me."

"Everyone is against me."

"I'm just too tired after working all week."

"I never thought about it."

"I don't know anyone."

"I can't just walk in and ask."

Steve Jobs, Cofounder of Apple Computer, Inc. – Dropped out of college to pursue computer interests.

Oprah Winfrey, Talk Show Host – In pursuit of television broadcasting interests, quit school prior to founding own Company and talk show.

Bill Gates, Cofounder of Microsoft Corporation – Richest person in the world several years running. Quit Harvard to follow his own interests.

Dave Thomas, founder of Wendy's – High School drop out.

Would you consider the foregoing individuals loser's or are they exceptions?

They are the examples. **Your point of beginning is less important than what you learn and apply during your journey.**

Surprisingly, there are many that lose sight of The Big Picture and many more that don't even have one.

The Big Picture is long term, long lasting and more important than short term or momentary perceived priorities. Gary leaves his sick daughter feeling obligated to attend a business associates wedding. He made the wrong decision and lost focus of his Big Picture realizing that the welfare of his daughter was something that was and always will be a part of his Big Picture and part of the rest of his life. The relationship of the business associate, although seemingly important at that moment, within a few months he no longer did any business with him. Gary has always regretted his having momentarily lost sight of the Big Picture.

The lesson I learned from this man was, when confronted with decisions, large and small, I would try to envision where I would be and what would be important years from now and the impact of the decision I needed to make today. In other words, make sure you have your mind and priorities focused upon your future (The Big Picture) and not just the moment (the small stuff).

Everyone has role models. Those role models may be intellectual, athletic, moral, spiritual, artistic, talented, musical, heroic, fearless, physically attractive, stylish, etc. We will naturally attempt to pattern ourselves and/or lifestyles to emulate these people. When confronted with a situation requiring a decision, what would those you admire do?

What would you do if you were the person you would like to be?

How often have you seen some variation of the following:

Young man wants to play professional basketball like Michael Jordan, but spends all of free time playing video games in his room.

Someone that wants to be like or perform like an athlete but makes no attempt to learn, take lessons, practice or exercise.

Someone that wants to have that 'perfect' body like a model but follows no diet or exercise program.

There are not too many successful people that simply woke up one morning without preparation, practice or training and immediately become successful athletes, business owners, business executives, artists, etc.

What would you do if you were the person you would like to be?

If you begin to lose sight of The Big Picture, step back and:
Remind yourself. What is it that you were ultimately trying to accomplish or achieve? What is your ultimate goal? Where are you trying to go?

Are you moving forward? Is your current action or direction moving you closer to achieving your Big Picture?

Have you lost direction? If you are not moving forward, what needs to change, happen or not happen. What steps need to be taken to get back on track?

Is this a Want or Need? Transportation is a need, a Porsche is a want. Identify and distinguish between wants and needs in your actions and choices.

What would I do? Think about what you would do if you were the person you wanted to be or were striving to become. What decision would you then make?

The Big Picture is mostly long term and, for most of us, would probably include the following:

Getting that much looked forward to car.
Graduating from school.
Finding that one perfect significant other, and having a loving relationship.
Personal safety.
Financial security.
Personal and family health.

Positive social relationships.
A rewarding and satisfying career.
Emotional and mental fulfillment.
A nice home.
To be happy.
Religious fulfillment.
Secured future.
Pursuit of personal interests and hobbies.
Healthy retirement.
Travel.

What are your Big Pictures?

Whatever they are, everything else is just the small stuff.

THE BIG PICTURE
and the small stuff

1. *See the big picture.* You must be able to visualize your Big Picture.
2. *Be flexible.* Your Big Picture can remain the same even if or when specifics or details change or evolve.
3. *Remind yourself* of what your goal(s) is, where you are going, what you are trying to achieve.
4. *Move forward.* Make sure actions move you closer to achievement.
5. *If not moving forward,* determine what needs to change. What steps must be taken to get back on track.
6. *Know the difference between wants and needs.*
7. *What would I do?* If you were the person you want to be or should be, then *"What would you do?"*

THE BOTTOM LINE

Staying focused on The Big Picture is necessary for success. The most important thing to remember is that your journey is more important than your beginning in reaching your Big Picture. If you lose sight of The Big Picture even if only for a moment, it could result not only in failure, but possibly irreversibly moving backwards. Make sure you take time to remind yourself of what your Big Picture is and if your actions are moving you forward or if you are spending time and energy going nowhere. Possibly the second most important single point in this chapter is to imagine the person you are striving to be when answering the oft asked question: *"What would I do?"*

A. Answer to previous chapter question.
"Mind like parachute – only function when open."
Charlie Chan at the Circus

CHAPTER THREE

Keep It Simple Stupid (KISS)

"Genius is the ability to reduce the complicated to the simple."

— C.W. Ceram

WEBSTER'S

"Having or composed of only one thing or part. Not complex."

MINE

"Reducing something to an improved and elementary state."

For most of us, the best way to improve the quality of your life is to simplify it.

To have more, bigger, faster, more elaborate, complex, taller, longer, a summer home, vacation home, weekend car, different color, more expensive, etc. This all contributes to life's complexities, anxieties, stress and pressures.

We all too often make a common mistake by thinking we need more and/or more expensive and valuable material possessions to be successful, the perception that *success equals stuff*. Those same material possessions work to complicate our lives. Less *stuff* means more time for life's purpose, life's relationships and enjoying life's freedoms.

According to studies, about 40 percent of us work an average of more than 50 hours per week. About 26 percent of workers take no vacations and almost two thirds of workers report being *"stressed out"*.

As simplicity expert Elaine St. James says, *"Maintaining a complicated life is a great way to avoid changing it."* It is easier to keep busy doing what you don't want to, working and living fast and hard rather than to stop and take time to figure out what you really want in your life: family, work, religious, social, hobbies, etc. Often, we don't even know what we want. Simplifying your life will provide you time to make a self assessment and answer those questions.

By simplifying your life, by eliminating those things that are distracting or nonproductive, you will free up your time and have energy to devote to the work and life that is important and that does matter. To have a great life you must know what that is and make and have the time for it.

We all have activities or relationships that demand time and energy but provide little to us in return. Eliminating unrewarding activities and avoiding the company of or obligation to a negative or energy sucking person or obligation will be rewarded with a more fulfilling life and more time for things that provide your life with a positive return.

The following steps will provide you some help.

Self evaluation. You must know what is really important to you. Too many apparently successful people in retrospect are actually ambivalent about their success because what they have acquired or achieved turns out not to be what they really wanted. They feel unfulfilled and empty and continue pursuing more of the same with the misguided belief that more is better but never really getting or achieving what they really want.

Time. Simplifying your life means taking control and creating more time to do what you want. According to a Time/CNN poll, 65% of people spend their leisure or free time doing something they really didn't want to do. Making more time will provide you the opportunity to really look at your life, marriage, family, friends, and work. Free up time every day and figure out what is complicating and draining your life and how you can change it. If you are working long hours, cut back. By reducing your work time a few hours per week you will probably discover that the things you really must do will still get done and you will simply be eliminating those things you probably didn't really need to do anyway. Change how you work not what you get done. With the extra time you find you can make an honest assessment of your marriage, family, friends, career, etc.

Restructuring your time, energy and financial resources into only those few activities that provide you the majority of your desired results. Become more efficient with the time you have and focus only on what is really important.

Live with less. Reduce your financial obligations. The more things you want, the more you must work to get them. The more you have, the more time you must devote to taking care of them. The less you have, the less you need to take care of. If you have a large home with lots of possessions, a vacation home, expensive cars and tastes, the more you must work to take care of it all. You create problems that require more of your time instead of reducing problems and making more time for you. Most people when asked what they would most like to have respond with, *"More time."* Ironically the more things you acquire in an attempt to satisfy yourself also are the same things preventing you from getting what you really want, *"More time."*

Knowing what you really need. Only acquire and hold on to those things you really need and use. If there are possessions in your home you haven't used over the last year or more, get rid of them. Don't acquire things that later fall into that category in the first place. Excluding antiques, mementos and keepsakes, of course.

Eliminate distractions that do not contribute to your simplified life. Distractions can drain up to 75% of your time and mental energy. That time and energy should be devoted to your desired and productive pursuits.

Learn to say "NO!" Playwright Jules Renard said, *"The truly free man is he who can decline a dinner invitation without giving an excuse."* Elaine St. James states, *"You can't lead a simple life if you can't say no."* She believes that no one can support more than three priorities. Work is one. Family is two. You must figure out what the third is. Simplicity is lost by over committing and over complicating your life by attempting to do more. Ms. St. James advice is, *"Figure out what your priorities are, and say no to everything else."* Making fewer commitments outside of your home and family means more time for what is important.

Assess and reinvent yourself. If you were a consultant reviewing your life, what recommendations, changes or advice would you make? Frequently review your life. Be open to new and changing priorities. Changes in life are inevitable. Priorities will change with changes in health, marriage, pregnancy, family, divorce, death, education, changes in career, technology, etc.; all will impact your life and cause you to reinvent yourself.

Consider the following example:

Two different wealthy couples concerned with estate planning to preserve wealth passed on to beneficiaries. The first couple spend $50,000 in legal, tax, accounting and financial planning fees to professionals. They establish multiple trusts that will require additional future fees for review and changes in laws and income taxes, at an estimated cost of $5,000 annually. The second couple purchase level term life insur-

ance policies at an annual cost of $2,500 the benefits for which will pay the income taxes for the beneficiaries in the event of their death. Couple two considered the cost/benefit and kept it simple.

This example may oversimplify the issue, however, points out a common problem. If you go to a surgeon, he is trained to resolve a problem with surgery. If you go to a trust attorney, their answer will be to set up trusts. You need to do your own self evaluation and assessment and decide what is simplest and works for you best.

Another example:

Jim is the owner of a Company with eight divisions. The CFO and accounting department provided to Jim and all the managers a two inch thick computer printout with income and expenses, categorized by each division. When I asked about specific Company overall income and expenses, no one, including Jim, knew the answer or could find it in their voluminous report. They had overcomplicated their reporting to ineffectiveness. I worked with the accounting department and their computer programmers to design and reprogram the system and structured a one page Company statement that reported total income and expenses by category while providing the answers Jim needed to make critical financial decisions for the Company as a whole.

To *"get a life"* you must take the time to make time. You must figure out how to make time for whatever you enjoy by taking time to assess what and how you are doing now.

Many people continue doing what they don't like or want to do because it's easier than figuring out what they want to do. Their *"success"* is empty and unrewarding.

Simplifying your life does not mean getting more help, but rather having fewer problems. Simplifying your life means taking control, eliminating distractions and having more time to figure out what really matters, and pursuing it.

Stan, a successful man in business worked twelve hour days, six days or more a week. With his commute, that left precious little or no time for family, and social activities were allowed only to the extent they perpetuated business interests. Upon meeting with a larger successful competitor he knew well and greatly respected, Stan opened his expanding briefcase and proudly removed a large stack of papers and files. *"These are all the files I need to keep track of my projects."* He declared, smiling with glee and pride looking for an impressed response from his friend. The friend removed a single small folded paper from his pocket with key information handwritten on it and responded, *"I only need this."* Stan suddenly realized that his friend had achieved simplified success where he had not. The friend needed only a small piece of paper to track the financial information that was important to him because wealth and power were reductive. Subordinates were delegated the burden and complexities of his wealth and ownership while he enjoyed a simple life.

KEEP IT SIMPLE STUPID

1. *Self evaluation* will find the answers to what is really important to you.

2. *Create more time* to do what you want and not what you don't want to do.

3. *Knowing what you want* and nothing more.

4. *Eliminate distractions* that do not contribute to your life.

5. *Learn to say "NO!"* To everything that is not one of your priorities.

6. *Assess and reinvent* your life and priorities as circumstances change.

THE BOTTOM LINE

It takes much less effort, time and wealth to support a simplified life. The benefits are received in the form of time for the pursuit of improved personal rewarding interests, spouse, family and friends. In addition, there will be less stress, pressure and anxiety with simplification which will translate to a healthier life. In today's world, there is much specialization which promotes these complexities, often unnecessary other than for self justification and benefit. Your mission is to overcome them and take control of your life, for your life's sake, and restore simplicity wherever possible.

Q. What movie are the following lines from?
(Government Agent) "We want to know what we should do."
"That's easy. Do what you do best.
Find something simple and complicate it."

CHAPTER FOUR

Positive Attitude and Lifestyle

"Think you can, think you can't; either way, you'll be right."

— Henry Ford

WEBSTER'S
*"Composed of or marked by a presence of distinctive qualities or attributes ...
(towards) a state of mind or feeling ... That reflects the values
and attitudes of an individual."*

MINE
*"Reinforcing and supportive state of mind, body, environment
and surroundings that is beneficial, healthy and constructive."*

In all aspects of Personal Success, ATTITUDE is a much more important ingredient for success than aptitude (knowledge). It has been established by many studies that eighty percent of your success is based upon attitude compared with only twenty percent on aptitude.

Some studies have even determined that attitude represents as high as eighty five to ninety percent of your success.

At any given point, your attitude is infectious to all exposed. Positive attitude will energize you and those around you. Negative attitude drains energy from you as well as from others.

Attitude is internal, a frame of mind and, therefore, totally within your own control and only affected by others to whatever degree you decide to let it be. It is not about what happens to a person but rather what a person lets happen.

To maintain a positive attitude, you need to recognize enemies that promote negative attitudes:

Exaggeration underestimates your own strengths and abilities and/or overestimates the situation, problem or challenge.

Over generalization of an isolated failure or the negative outcome and extending it to all similar and future possible endeavors.

Personalizing is believing everything is about you.

Ultimatums about achievement. For example: "If I don't get that job, I'm such a failure."

False assumptions in explaining why things don't go your way.

Always looking for the negative of an outcome instead of focusing on the positive.

The attitude of others will affect you if you let it. If theirs is positive, let it, if negative, ignore it.

Brian Tracy in his program *"21 Success Secrets of Self Made Millionaires"* states that *"By using your mind, your ability to think, you become a creator of circumstances rather than a creature of circumstances. You move from being powerless to being powerful. ... You may not be what you think you are, but what you think, you are!"*

Psychologist William James of Harvard wrote, *"The greatest revolution of my generation is the discovery that individuals, by changing their inner attitudes of mind, can change the outer aspects of their lives."*

A person with an unstoppable positive mental attitude is knowledgeable, presents themselves effectively, maintains a calm confident presence and exudes optimistic enthusiasm and success.

A positive attitude can be developed and learned by remembering the following tips:

Nobody's perfect. Not being perfect is not failing, it's being human.

Confidence and contentment in the self knowledge that you are making your best possible effort and what you do you are good at and others will know, appreciate and recognize this also.

There are no failures. All outcomes, especially those that were less than expected or hoped for, are an opportunity to learn. By learning, no matter what the outcome, you have succeeded.

Your appearance should receive the attention it deserves by generating a positive self image while lifting your spirits and reinforcing your confidence.

Your language should reflect the positive. How often are you successful at something or win after telling yourself you can't do it? First: be aware of your language. Second: replace the negative with the positive.

Positive thoughts during the day will help reinforce positive language and actions leading to positive results.

Diffuse anger. Anthony Robbins in his book "Awaken the Giant Within" describes how he lowered the intensity of his anger by altering his language. For example, instead of saying he was "angry and upset," he chose to say, "I feel myself getting a bit peeved."

Strengthen your language with a powerful vocabulary. For example, when greeted with "How are you doing?" Instead of answering "Good" answer "I'm doing really great today!"

The Future will be built on the foundations of the present. The past cannot be changed.

Having a positive attitude means being part of the solution and not part of the problem.

Don't be concerned about what others think. As someone once said, "Those who mind don't matter and those who matter don't mind."

Take time for you. Psychiatrist Theodore I. Rubin writes, "A day devoted to ourselves – no strings attached – can be a wonderful morale booster. This is not selfishness; it is just good mental health."

Consider the following poem, *"The Set of the Sails"* written by Rebecca R. Williams:

"One ship drives east and another west,
With the self-same winds that blow;
'Tis the set of the sails and not the gales
That determines where they go.
Like the winds of the sea are the ways of fate,
As we voyage along through life;
'Tis the set of a soul that decides the goal –
And not the calm or the strife."

Norman Cousins was afflicted with a crippling arthritic disease causing disintegrating spinal connective tissue, for which there was no cure or recovery. He discovered that by a change in his attitude he actually laughed himself to health.

Mr. Cousins concluded a 12 year study with 2,000 individuals reporting the results in his book *Anatomy of an Illness.* Upon diagnosis of a disease or affliction, a patient became worse off than if they had not been diagnosed. Their mental awareness affected their attitude and they actually accelerated the disease's affects.

A branch of medicine known as psychoneuroimmunology (no kidding!) is the study and application of the relationship between positive mental attitude and physical health. It has clearly established that a positive attitude results in faster recovery from surgery, disease, illness, higher resistance to arthritis and cancer, and a stronger immune system.

How can this be? Glad you asked. The body produces neuropeptides that directs your immune system. A positive attitude directs more production and a negative attitude or depression reduces that direction.

Dr. Jonathan Whiteson of *NYU Medical Center* tracks and studies recovery in heart attack and heart surgery patients. The study concluded that pessimistic patients had more heart related deaths and overall deaths than patients who were optimists. He states, *"Those with better mood and optimism have shorter length of stay, fewer complications, make greater functional improvements."*

The University of Texas concluded a seven year study on aging frailty that showed the effects of aging were affected by psychosocial factors (positive attitude and emotions). An optimistic person was less frail than a pessimistic person as they age. Researchers stated that, *"...our thoughts and attitudes/emotions affect physical functioning, and over all health..."*

In a test on memory, a study by North Carolina State University of people of varying ages were presented with a selection of positive and negative words. The overall memory performance was lower when confronted with negative words and higher when presented with positive words and the study determined that age was not a factor.

According to H. Howard in *Updating Estimates of the Economic Costs of Alcohol Abuse in the United States,* an estimated $184 BILLION is spent on alcohol related health problems each year.

According to the *United States Center for Disease Control* (1995-1999) an estimated $62 BILLION is spent by the Federal and State Governments on smoking related health problems each year.

According to the *Schaffer Library of Drug Policy* (1993) an estimated $400 BILLION is spent on drug abuse related problems each year.

According to the *Center for Disease Control and Prevention,* obesity related health issues cost about $75 billion during 2003. About $39 billion was paid through Medicare and Medicaid. Obesity accounts for an average of 5% of the budgets of all the states medical care. An estimated 64% of citizens in the United States are overweight or obese.

Your health and lifestyle contribute to your attitude. If you don't feel well, if you are continually battling sickness, addictions, illness or disease, you are probably not going to be able to maintain a very good attitude.

A positive attitude and lifestyle will favorably impact your emotions and health and that of everyone you come into contact with. You must train yourself to avoid conditions and persons that might thwart your positive efforts and focus your efforts on maintaining your positive attitude.

With a Positive Attitude and Lifestyle, you can achieve *Personal Success.*

CREATING NEGATIVE ATTITUDE

1. *Exaggerating* the situation, problem or challenge.
2. *Over generalization* of outcomes.
3. *Personalizing* everything being about you.
4. *Setting ultimatums* on yourself.
5. *Making false assumptions.*
6. *Always looking for the negative.*
7. *Letting others attitudes have a negative affect.*

KEEPING A POSITIVE ATTITUDE

1. *Being imperfect* is not only all right, but inevitable.
2. *Be confident* in your best possible effort and your abilities.
3. *You never fail.* You always have opportunity to learn.
4. *Your appearance* reflects your own self image.
5. *You language* should always be positive.
6. *Your thoughts* should always be positive.
7. *Replace anger* in your thoughts and language.
8. *Strengthen your language* to reflect your positive attitude.
9. *Your future* is based upon the choices of your present actions.
10. *Be a problem solver,* not a problem maker.
11. *It's what you think* that is important.
12. *Make time for yourself.*

POSITIVE LIFESTYLE

1. *The better you feel, the better your attitude.*
2. *The better your attitude, the better you feel.*
3. *A positive attitude affects your health, positively.*
4. *Laughter really is the best medicine.*

THE BOTTOM LINE

Attitude has more impact than aptitude. With a positive attitude you can move mountains. With a negative attitude you will be crushed by them. Your attitude and the attitude of others will greatly impact your life if you let it. Let your positive attitude out and seek out those who share theirs. Negative attitude, yours and others, should not be a part of your life.

A positive lifestyle will affect your attitude and success. Time and resources are wasted on the affects of avoidable negative health. Those who aggressively pursue success also aggressively pursue health.

A. Answer to previous chapter question.
(Government Agent) "We want to know what we should do."
"That's easy. Do what you do best.
Find something simple and complicate it."
Tremors III – Back to Perfection

Q. What movie is the following line from?
"Old age. It's the only disease, Mr. Thompson, that you don't
look forward to being cured of."

CHAPTER   FIVE

Accepting Responsibility

*"A man may fall many times, but he won't be a
failure until he says someone pushed him."*

— Elmer G. Letterman

WEBSTER'S

Responsible *"Capable of making moral or rational decisions
on one's own, thereby being answerable for one's behavior."*
"Involving personal accountability..."

MINE

*"Accepting and acknowledging accountability for the results of
your own decisions, choices, actions or inaction without
directing fault to others for unfavorable outcomes."*

You cannot achieve personal success when your defense
mechanism is to blame others for your own life's problems or failures.

Human nature is to not blame yourself but rather to point the
finger at and blame someone else for your failure. You have probably

heard (certainly not used) one or more of the following common defensive claims:

> *"It's not my fault."*
> *"It wasn't my job."*
> *"John didn't give me enough time."*
> *"No one called me."*
> *"They didn't try hard enough."*
> *"They didn't want me to (insert your own)."*
> *"No one contacted me."*
> *"I didn't have enough information."*
> *"No one told me to."*
> *"There wasn't enough money."*
> *"They took too long to check me in and I missed the plane."*
> *"The line was too long and it made me late."*
> *"I'm late because I got caught in traffic."*
> *"My girlfriend got pregnant."*
> *"The dog ate my papers."*

Many professionals leach a living from their clients by deflecting fault and assigning failure externally, finding if not creating a reason to blame others for the results of actions or inactions that damaged their clients or caused their clients to do or not do whatever. Noteworthy inexplicable coincidence, the person or company the attorney's find to blame seem to usually have the best insurance or greatest financial resources.

Real life examples:

> *Lady sues fast food giant for burn caused from her spilling recently purchased coffee into her lap.*

Lady sues fast food giant for obesity of herself and child blaming food products not healthy.

HIV positive drug addict, infected by a shared and infected needle, sues Health Authorities for their failure to provide him with clean needles even though Health Authorities don't supply needles at all to illegal drug addicts.

Man sues amusement park for injuries sustained during his after hours break in and usage of rides.

Man sues property owner for injuries sustained when falling through roof during attempted burglary.

Woman sues gun manufacturer for death of husband shot by intruder during home invasion.

Woman sues law enforcement authorities for death of husband killed when his car wrecked trying to escape from police during a chase by authorities following his armed robbery of store.

Man sues credit card Company for excessive outstanding unpaid balance citing their irresponsibility for issuing him a high credit limit.

Man arrested at fast food restaurant after assaulting employees and police over restaurant being out of French fries and losing temper. His defense was that the restaurant was at fault.

Blaming others becomes habit forming and addictive. It is a disservice to yourself and you become a bad leader and role model to and for others. Your significant other will most likely not forgive you. Your coworkers will not respect or trust you. Your children will learn from you and grow up to be like you.

If you cannot be honest with yourself, how can anyone else possibly expect you to be honest and trustworthy with them?

If you cannot be honest with yourself and accept responsibility how can you learn? If you believe you have done nothing wrong, there is no opportunity for learning.

From my observations and supported by noted Psychologist Saul Rosensweig's work, in summary there are three responses for assigning blame: **External, Internal and No Fault.**

External is to cast the blame on others resulting in anger directed towards them. Since I did nothing wrong, therefore it was obviously all their fault.

Internal is to always blame yourself for everything. This results in low self esteem, guilt and humiliation.

No fault is thoughtful and assigns fault to a source outside the control of yourself or others.

For example, if you leave a message for someone on a recorder and do not receive a return call, the **External** individual will think that person rude, snobbish or intentionally avoiding them. The **Internal** individual will wonder what they did wrong and wonder if the other person is upset or mad with them. The **No Fault** individual will look for a cause, such as, the message must have been accidentally erased and not received, a family member failed to pass the message on, the person may be out of town, etc.

External and **Internal** responses are aggressive either towards others or yourself and not quickly forgotten. Both responses will be remembered unfavorably. In contrast, the **No Fault** response is quickly forgotten without any aggression.

Certainly, **No Fault** responses are preferred, relieving yourself of aggression and any future dwelling on the issue.

You can overcome blaming others for your failures by learning the following traits of a successful person:

Self awareness. Be aware when you start to blame others for your own poor performance or life failures.

Honesty. Be honest with yourself. If you failed to do or not do something, be honest. This does not mean others are never responsible, but rather honestly assess your own actions and failings.

Don't react, respond. External and Internal are reactive responses. To respond with No Fault is avoiding any aggression and is quickly forgotten.

Value relationships. Blaming others for your own life problems, failures, performance or consequences will damage if not destroy relationships and create distrust and estrangement from others.

Set an example. Accepting responsibility for your own decisions and actions, and the results provides a good example for others and builds credibility and trust. You will earn respect and build valuable friendships and alliances.

Failure is:

Inevitable

A teaching and learning opportunity.

Acceptable.

A predecessor to success.

A beginning, not an end.

Human.

Accepting responsibility is to:

Accept that the decisions and choices you make are yours and yours alone.

Acknowledge that you are solely responsible for the choices and decisions you make during your life.

Accept that you have chosen where your life's direction is going.

Accept that others are not to blame for all negative results or outcomes from your decisions or choices.

Not depend on others to feel good about yourself.

Abandon hostility or anger towards others over the past.

NOT accepting responsibility is to:

Blame others for your own failures.

Blame others for negative outcomes from your actions or decisions.

Fail at establishing positive personal relationships.

Rely on unhealthy self destructive substances or activities.

Not acknowledge fault.

Be angry, hostile and/or depressed.

Foster paranoia.

Believe you cannot change or make changes.

When things aren't what you expect or want them to be, honestly look inside you first to answer what went wrong. What did or didn't you do? Could you have done something that would have made a positive difference? What action or decision could have been different? Were you inattentive or complacent? Who could have made a difference and how could you have dealt with them? Was my personal effort deficient? Was I not paying attention? What did I miss? Did I dedicate my time and resources to the issue or gloss over it relying totally on others?

Listen to your answers and apply yourself to not making the same mistake twice.

ACCEPTING RESPONSIBILITY

1. *Self awareness* is recognizing when you are blaming others for your own failures.
2. *Be honest* with yourself and with others.
3. *Respond with thought* instead of reacting without thinking.
4. *Value relationships* by not blaming others for your problems. Otherwise those relationships will probably never recover.
5. *Set an example* for others and build trust, respect and credibility.
6. *Failure can be a positive or a negative.* It's your choice.
7. *Your life's decisions and choices are yours* and yours alone, and the results are solely your own doing.
8. *Only you are responsible* for your life's direction.
9. *Failure to accept responsibility will cause you to:*
   Blame Others
   Destroy good relationships
   Promote anger, hostility, depression and resentment
   Foster paranoia

   FAIL TO ACHIEVE PERSONAL SUCCESS.

THE BOTTOM LINE

When making your decisions and choices, always give them the attention needed and deserved. Directing blame elsewhere later is unacceptable. Own up to your actions and decisions whether the results are good or bad. Your life is a result of there outcome, favorable or not, and not anyone else's fault. The only one to blame when there is failure is you. By accepting and taking responsibility, you will respect yourself and earn the respect of others who will also learn by example. They already know who is responsible, and are simply waiting to assess your character.

"A man who refuses to admit his mistakes
can never be successful.
But if he confesses and forsakes them,
he gets another chance."

— Proverbs 28:13 (TLB)

A. Answer to previous chapter question.
"Old age. It's the only disease, Mr. Thompson,
That you don't look forward to being cured of."
Citizen Kane

Q. What movie is the following line from?
"First rule of leadership: Everything is your fault."

CHAPTER SIX

Self Motivation and Commitment

"Great men undertake great things because they are great; fools, because they think them easy."

— Vauvenargues

WEBSTER'S
"Motivate – *"To provide with an incentive."*
Commitment – *"The state of being bound emotionally or intellectually to an ideal or course of action."*

MINE
"A recognized need or desire for change bonded with an unstoppable drive to achieve the change that cannot be deterred."

Having and sustaining your motivation and commitment can be difficult, but it is absolutely essential. You must have both in order to formulate your goals, initiate, monitor and modify your plans, and achieve **Personal Success.**

Motivation is born from the recognition that a change must occur to satisfy a designated need or desire.

Motivation is an internal state of mind that functions as the catalyst for a change in behavior, persistence of behavior, actions and direction.

For a brief clinical explanation:

A variation to Victor Vroom's <u>expectancy theory</u> equation of motivation from his book *Work and Motivation*, is:

Motivation = Expectation of achievement x
Capability to succeed x
Value of achievement

Since Vroom established that each factor is multiplied by the other, any low value in one results in a lower overall degree of motivation. Therefore, each variable must be high and remain high in order to have and sustain motivation.

If expected achievement is reduced, overall motivation is reduced or eliminated. If your capability is reduced, overall motivation is reduced or eliminated. If the value is reduced, overall motivation is reduced or eliminated.

Consider the following steps that create and sustain motivation:

Be discontent. To be receptive to the need or desire for change, you must be discontent with existing or achieved needs or desires.

Establish your well planned goals. Having goals provides for the introduction of opportunity. Having clear and detailed well thought through plans will keep your motivation from faltering.

Complete your plan and goal. Completing your plan and achieving your goal becomes a habit. So does losing motivation and quitting.

Be able to visualize your goals. Be able to see the completion of your goals and the value that you will receive.

Create a mutual support system. Socialize with others of like interests and/or goals. You will accomplish more and you will accomplish it faster with a mutual support system and will learn something from others.

Avoid destructive relationships. If you associate with unmotivated losers, you will tend to become one. Avoid those that fail to see, understand, appreciate or accept the reality of your motivation.

Learn from others but mostly yourself. We can always learn from others, however, you must be individually creative and establish your own dreams, not those of others.

Believe you can succeed. Belief in your ability to succeed will sustain motivation just as much as believing you cannot will cause you to fail.

Learn to fail in order to succeed. Most worthwhile significant success' are the result of learning after several failures. Failure is merely a learning tool, not always but often necessary before achieving success.

Balance interest with ability. Motivation is born from talent and ability which creates perseverance. Your interests' will be guided by your abilities.

Perseverance. There are no failures, only opportunities to learn another way to succeed. Thomas Edison failed many times before persevering to success. Any perceived failure is just a temporary state.

Motivation should always be kept positive to prevent successful self destruction.

Certainly you want to avoid cutting someone off in traffic to get even for them having cut you off. The correct motivation would be to create a distance between them and you so that you don't get involved in a possible accident that they might cause thereby avoiding injury to yourself and others.

Motivation is the vehicle, Commitment is the engine.

Consider the following factors that contribute to increased and sustained commitment.

High degree of personal responsibility. Being personally responsible contributes to the quality of final work product that is specifically and personally associated with you.

High degree of autonomy. Commitment is sustained when you are autonomous and can work at your own pace without having to report to, be directed by or answer to another or conform to their schedule.

Your work must be personally satisfying. You must receive personal satisfaction from your work accomplishments.

A high quality of personal interactive relationships. Work with others of high caliber capabilities, morals, abilities, etc.

Fair personal assessments. A fair assessment from others is important for sustained commitment.

There are several factors that will reduce commitment.

Ambiguous goals or plans. Goals or plans that are not clear or well thought out and specific will create frustration, failure and loss of time, energy and motivation.

Stress or tension. Stress or tension in carrying out plans will reduce commitment within yourself and others.

Lack of others support or understanding. If others fail to be supportive and understanding of your goals and plans, you will lose your commitment.

Not correctly quoted, but when Thomas Edison was asked how he was able to remain committed to making a light bulb after about two thousand failures, he responded, *"There were no failures. I simply discovered two thousand ways to not make a light bulb."*

Interpreting and summarizing a University of Washington study by Elizabeth Miller, doctoral candidate in psychology and Alan Marlatt, director of the University's Addictive Behaviors Research Center that includes more than 20 years of research, for there to be success:

There must be:

> Strong persevering commitment.
> Planning strategies that include dealing with problems.
> Tracking of progress.

Failure results when,

> There is poor planning or a lack of planning.
> Reactive decisions based on emotions or thoughts at that moment without overall consideration for long term impact.

According to Ms. Miller, *"The keys to making a successful resolution are ... the commitment to making that change."*

In their study of 264 subjects making health related New Year's Eve resolutions, 60 percent failed to achieve their top resolution on the first attempt with another 17 percent being successful only after six or more failures.

There is a difference in commitment level related to doing something you are excited about and want to do or doing something because you have to (compliance). This should especially be kept in mind in dealing with others that are needed to be involved when committing to and achieving your goals.

If others participate in defining your goals and developing your plan or even possibly personally benefiting from your achievement, they will be committed to your success as opposed to simply performing their designated roles.

An overweight out of shape person that is initially motivated, joins a spa to lose weight and tone up. After a few weeks of disciplined participation and some success, she finds reasons to go less frequently until she stops completely after a few more weeks. She had lost her commitment.

Cyndi has long been an overweight person that frequently tries to lose weight beginning every new diet that comes along. Quickly, Cyndi returned to her former eating habits for whatever reason and orders a diet Coke with her cheeseburger, French fries and chocolate sundae. If Cyndi ever really had commitment, she had certainly lost it.

Delores, an overweight grandmother was told by her Doctor that her condition put her at serious risk of death from heart disease. After two years of a healthy diet and exercise program, she achieved proper weight, blood pressure, cholesterol levels and heart health. To stay motivated Delores always kept two pictures in her purse. The first one was when she was overweight in a bathing suit. The second picture was of her three grandchildren that she feared she would not live long enough to watch them grow up if she had not changed her lifestyle. This is how Delores kept motivated and committed.

A small and once profitable and successful mother and daughter owned business was now losing money. They recognized they had a problem and were motivated to the point of meeting with a business expert and they developed and all agreed to a fifteen item list outlining actions needed to return the business to profitability. After three months, the business expert contacts them for a follow up meeting. Upon meeting with the mother and daughter, he discovered that not one item on the list had been completed by either the mother or daughter. Only one item had even been started. Their business continued to lose money. Neither was committed to their business success and insolvency and bankruptcy soon followed.

MOTIVATION

1. *Be discontent.*
2. *Establish your well planned goals.*
3. *Complete your plan.*
4. *Visualize your goals.*
5. *Keep motives positive.*
6. *Create support system.*
7. *Avoid destructive relationships.*
8. *Learn from others but mostly from yourself.*
9. *Believe you can succeed.*
10. *Learn to fail in order to succeed.*
11. *Balance interest with ability.*
12. *Perseverance.*

COMMITMENT

1. *You must have a high degree of personal responsibility.*
2. *You must have autonomy.*
3. *It must be personally satisfying.*
4. *You should have a high quality of interactive relationships.*
5. *You must receive fair assessments.*

Failure is caused by:

1. *Making ambiguous goals or plans.*
2. *Creating stress or tension.*
3. *The lack of support or understanding from others.*

THE BOTTOM LINE

Motivation precedes and fuels commitment. Ultimately, the degree of success is directly proportional to the degree of commitment. Fragmented failures provide opportunities to learn and practice perseverance. Seeing something through to completion is learned and will become a habit that you should begin as early as possible. Positive motives should always replace negative motives.

Motivation without commitment is like walking on a treadmill. The faster you move, the faster you go nowhere.

A. Answer to previous chapter question.

"First rule of leadership:

Everything is your fault."

A Bug's Life

CHAPTER SEVEN

Self Confidence

"All you need in this life is ignorance and confidence; then success is sure."

— Mark Twain

W E B S T E R ' S
"A feeling of self assurance."

M I N E
*"Continued positive self recognition of ability regardless
of outcome or opinions of others."*

In this discussion, you may consider the issues addressing low self confidence synonymous with low self esteem.

Identify any individual that is successful and you will most certainly have identified someone that has self confidence.

Self confidence is the belief in your own ability to accomplish what you plan and achieve expected results while maintaining control over your own life.

Self confidence is measuring up to your own realistic standards and results and not the realistic or unrealistic standards or results that others might want to impose on you.

Self confidence consists of a combination of ability, assertiveness, self awareness, risk acceptance, compassion, perpetual optimism, trust, independence and the ability to handle criticism and assess your own strengths, abilities and limitations.

Self confident people have realistic expectations and are willing to take risks and trust their own abilities not fearing the possible realization of disapproval from others that might attempt to deter them.

The absence of self confidence results in self doubt, passiveness, submission, isolation, being overly sensitive to criticism, distrust, depression, belief of inferiority, feeling unloved or unwanted, and leads to successive failures. People without self confidence must depend on the approval of others instead of themselves to feel good. They often put themselves down, mentally and verbally and discount compliments paid to them by others. These people in general do not take risks for fear of failure, do not believe they can be and, in fact, are not successful.

Self confidence is attained and measured over time with the successful completion of and benefits achieved from reaching personal performance goals.

A lack of self confidence will prevent you from taking risks because of a fear to fail, self doubt or negative thinking. A person with low or no self confidence will often blame themselves for failure even when the fault is outside their control and/or caused by others.

Overconfidence can put you into a position or situation you are not capable of handling and may not be able to get out of. This can cause serious failure and critically damage future self confidence.

Overconfidence can be caused by vanity, ego and failure to recognize the inability or inappropriate pressure of others.

"You never know until you try." — Unknown

Most of us won't even consider asking. Those who succeed do so often simply because they asked.

Successful people usually have at least two common traits:

First – *They love being challenged.*

Second – *The more successful are the more charitable.*

Since they are successful, money is no longer a motivation, if it ever was.

For example, to speculate, let's assume that you were a new young developer trying to develop a parcel of real estate in New York City and had a never before encountered problem or situation that seemed insurmountable.

A person with no self confidence would probably never even imagine much less consider approaching Donald Trump. Most of us could not afford Donald Trump's time, even if it were available, however, a self confident person might approach him and ask for his help with the challenge. You may still not be given any of his time but I bet he would at least consider it. What have you got to lose?

There have been many times when successful people at the forefront of their field have provided assistance or expertise simply for the challenge and/or the charity. Over the years I have provided services gratis when the individual or situation warranted it, <u>because they simply asked me</u>.

Ken and Elisa are a young married couple with five children and they had saved and purchased a new home. Ken works for UPS and has a truck route. One of his customers is a successful interior designer, Andrew. Ken has had friendly conversations with Andrew and told him about their home. Ken asked Andrew if he would consider stopping by and possibly giving them some decorating tips. Andrew new that Ken and Elisa couldn't afford him but smiled and said he would be happy to, at no charge. Arriving at their home, Andrew was greeted by Ken, and Elisa had prepared some snacks and drinks. Andrew was so impressed by the young couples appreciation that he ended up spending a couple hours and went through every room providing them with expert decorating information. He provided his services for free because they simply asked him.

A study by Harvard University showed that only 3% of a graduating class had the confidence to develop, write down and pursue their written goals. They followed these graduates for 30 years. The result: After thirty years the 3% of the people that had written goals and had the confidence to pursue and act upon them had amassed financial fortunes that exceeded the entire 97% of the remaining graduates combined!

Low or no self confidence is developed and perpetuated by:

Self consciousness. This is recognized by many as the primary reason for low self confidence. When you feel yourself becoming anxious, get your attention off yourself and focus it onto something or someone else.

Fear of failure. The fear of failing and/or being criticized by others results in the fear of doing or even trying.

Perfection. Expecting perfection from yourself and requiring the approval of others without recognizing a valuable learning opportunity and if you are unable to accept criticism as constructive leads to low self confidence. An all or nothing frame of mind is harmful.

Prior experience. A negative experience in your past reinforced by criticism from family, friends, coach, school mates, etc. that resulted in your own negative perception of yourself.

The loss of someone emotionally close such as a parents death or divorce, moving away from home or a broken or ended relationship.

Dwelling on the negative. If you always are looking for the negative, the worst or the dark clouds or are always the pessimist.

Inability to overcome failure. Not being able to learn, forget and move on.

Undue criticism. If you believe your own criticism and/or the criticism of others, not viewing is as constructive. We are always hardest on ourselves.

Exaggeration. Believing something is worse than it really is.

Unrealistic goals. If you fail to realistically assess your own abilities.

Self confidence can be learned or improved by:

Taking risks. Be confident in your own ability and in recognizing an opportunity for new experiences and possibilities to learn. Not doing so is in itself a failure and a stagnation of personal achievement and growth.

Always think positive about yourself. If you think or call yourself stupid, ugly, worthless or uncoordinated then you will start believing it and most likely become so, when you weren't before.

Have a realistic assessment of your abilities. No one is great at everything. Identify and recognize your strengths and weaknesses. Exploit your strengths and improve or avoid your weaknesses. Accept that perfection is not possible in everything that you do.

Personal identity. Pressure from others to meet their demands or expectations will suppress development of your own identity, independence and freedom. Don't be afraid to be yourself instead of what others want or think you should be.

Reward yourself. Reward yourself for your achievements with a bottle of champagne, vacation, personal getaway, etc.

Rational assessment. Make honest rational assessments of your situation and do not base those assessments on emotions.

Be assertive. Don't be afraid to express your feelings, opinions, thoughts, beliefs and needs openly and honestly, and without fear of criticism or retribution. Don't be afraid to say "No" or voice your disagreement when it is warranted.

Evaluation. Your evaluation is the only one that matters. You do not require the approval of others to achieve.

There are people that will want to suppress a potentially self confident person in order to create or extend their control over them and establish pseudo dependence. Often these people will attempt to supplement their own inadequacies by suppressing the self confident person. They will do this by becoming louder, be verbally or physically abusive, use body language, proximity or posture to intimidate, be verbally abusive and/or insulting with non stop narrative. These are people that can only be happy through their control and assuring the misery of others. Get away from them if you can, ignore them if you can't, but most certainly do not let them exert their influence upon you.

In relationships, there are people that will exploit low self confidence and low self esteem to their advantage. A person who is insecure and afraid of failing in a relationship or being left by the other, will seek out an individual with low self esteem. A person with low self esteem will feel they are worthless, inferior and will be submissive. They believe they are unwanted and unloved and will cling to whatever they have no matter how physically or emotionally abusive and oppressive the relationship is.

Confidence can be degraded with time and effort. Constantly telling someone they are fat, unattractive and unwanted by anyone else, living with a dysfunctional relationship that is believed to be the best the person can achieve, entrapping them and preventing them from searching for a truly loving and nourishing relationship.

If you are lucky, you live in an environment that is supportive, encouraging and strengthening in self confidence. If not, start training yourself and seek others that will be supportive and help you to establish your self confident environment. This is critical to develop and the sooner you begin, the sooner you can master it and achieve Personal Success.

Awareness is the diagnosis.

Action is the surgery.

Implementation is the recovery.

Self confidence is the cure.

Personal Success is the benefit.

Acceptance of failure is the difference between achievers and wannabe's. John C. Maxwell of The Injoy Group and author of several books has a sign in his office, *"Yesterday ended last night."* His advice is to *"View failure as something that happened in the past."* Each day is a new day with new possibilities and opportunities. What happened yesterday is history.

There is never a guarantee of success and, therefore, failure is always possible.

Handle any failure as:

Inevitable and a learning opportunity.

You will fail again, unless you don't try.

You are not a failure, simply someone who has failed at something.

If you never fail, you have stopped challenging yourself.

If you repeatedly fail at the same thing, you may not be learning.

The difference between failure and success may only be inches and not yards. Don't stop trying.

PROMOTING LOW OR NO SELF CONFIDENCE OR SELF ESTEEM

1. *Self consciousness.* When you feel yourself becoming anxious, stressed or nervous and that everyone is watching and criticizing.

2. *Fear of failure* prevents you from even trying.

3. *Expectations of perfection* and only accepting perfection from yourself.

4. *Prior experiences.* A negative past experience especially when reinforced with open or public criticism.

5. *Loss of someone close to you* by death, divorce, rejection, ended relationship, a move.

6. *Dwelling on the negative* instead of accepting it as merely a passing learning experience.

7. *Inability to overcome failure* to learn, forget and move forward.

8. *Undue criticism* from yourself or others.

9. *Exaggeration* that it is worse than it is.

10. *Unrealistic goals* set in the beginning.

11. *Others* may wish to keep or make your self confidence or self esteem low for their own personal benefit or gain. If you know or deal with this type of person, avoid them, get away from them quickly.

BUILDING
SELF CONFIDENCE

1. *Taking risks.* Be confident in your own abilities and recognize the learning value of risk taking. Nothing ventured, nothing gained. Just ask and try.
2. *Always think positive,* especially about yourself.
3. *Make realistic assessments* of your own abilities identifing your strengths and recognizing your weaknesses.
4. *Your personal identity* is what you are and what you make it, not what others want it to be.
5. *Reward yourself* for your achievements.
6. *Make rational assessments* of your decisions, actions, results and achievements.
7. *Be assertive* in expressing your feelings, beliefs, opinions and emotions, openly and honestly and without fear of criticism or retribution. You are just as important as an one else. (More so than stupid people!)
8. *Your self evaluation* is the only one that matters. You do not require the approval of others.

THE BOTTOM LINE

To be self confident is to be successful. Make an honest self assessment and measure your own level of self confidence. If it is less than what it should be try the following:

First: Identify what characteristics that you have learned or developed that contribute to low self confidence. See previous list.

Second: Identify what about your environment is destructive to your self confidence. It might be an unsupportive spouse, family, friends, coworkers or social relationships.

Third: Decide what you must do to change those destructive forces.

Fourth: Change them. Internal forces can change with awareness, time and positive replacements. Change the external forces that you can and eliminate those that you can't change.

Fifth: Be successful.

Q. What movie is the following line from?

"Come on in, and try not to ruin everything by being you."

CHAPTER EIGHT

Being Competitive

"When you want to win a game, you have to teach.
When you lose a game, you have to learn."

— Tom Landry

WEBSTER'S
"To strive or contend, as for profit or a prize."

MINE
"The drive to be the best or first and enthusiastically
pursue and thrive on the competition."

Successful people are competitors that understand the difference first in the science of competition, where many competitors stop, but more importantly they understand and practice the art of competition.

The science of competition involves research and discovery, networking information and utilizing available technologies and resources.

The art of competition, which is a learned and developed skill over time, requires observation, intelligent interpretation of results, accurate prediction, acting and reacting with confidence to direct and achieve desired results.

Let's first review some competitive guidelines:

You compete against a person. Know who you are competing against. Decisions are ultimately made by one person, whether in a Company, group, team or family. Know who makes that decision because regardless who else may be involved, your understanding of the decision makers motivations, issues, thought processes, strategies, procedures and concerns will help you in your cause.

Isolate the important information. You will accumulate much data and information that will be unimportant, note-worthy or important. You need to distinguish what is important and what is not so you can focus energy, time, money and resources only on what is important. The more verification or substantiation of the important information, the better you avoid wasting time and resources.

Efficiency. Your processes must be as efficient as possible in isolating the important information to avoid paralysis and failure from a delayed action or reaction. Opportunity lost from a delayed response while attempting to analyze every single piece of information and reviewing all possible alternatives or responses in a time when so much information is readily available has defeated many a competitor.

Many think that to be a good competitor means to control or defeat your opponent. To win as defined by a score, making the sale, putting them out of business, protagonist versus antagonist, going to whatever degree is needed to totally destroy the other person, an *"Us versus them"* or *"Me against you"* mentality.

However, consider the following definition of a competitor.

A good competitor is a teacher from which you will learn from and, in turn, you will also teach. In this respect, you will view competition in a very positive light.

Consider the American automobile industry in the 1980's, complacent with product development and improvement to the degree that it allowed foreign manufacturers to enter the market and rapidly seize significant market share by making a higher quality more dependable product. That foreign competition forced the American automobile manufacturers to learn from their *"Teachers"* resulting in the acceleration of their own product improvement.

The successful person's goal is not necessarily just to beat their competitors, but also to view them as teachers and learn what they are doing right which will result in you becoming an even stronger competitor than before. If you have learned from your competition, then you have won, regardless of the end result.

Counterproductive competition results from internal competition. For example, in a team sport, if you are competing against a teammate or a teammate against you as a rival, opponent or even enemy, this results in a divisive team and probable defeat. If energy is devoted to competition between teammates, that energy is distracted from defeating your opponent.

If competing against a colleague, you or they will withhold knowledge or information and jeopardize personal and/or company gains.

If you capitalize on diversity to combine talents and resources, utilize individual strengths to compensate for personal weaknesses, use competition within yourself and others to teach and learn, a formidable force will be created.

How to become a competitive teacher and student:

> *Change your view.* A good competitor can teach you much. Your goal is not necessarily just to defeat or win, but also to learn and become a better competitor. Good competitors that are simply looking only to win will ultimately be defeated by a better competitor.

> *Measurement.* Measure your results against the best of others no matter who they are, where they are or what it is.

> *Form alliances.* Former competitors can become strong or strategic allies. Common interests, visions, goals, purpose or opponents can compliment your strengths and compensate for your weaknesses.

> *Stay centered.* Your actions and methods will be whatever you center on. If you center on negatives like only money, revenge, greed, etc. you will lose principles and positive relationships. You may become paranoid and begin to view everyone as either for you or against you, creating enemies when there should not have been.

> *Learn.* Lose the arrogance and ego. Find the benefits of learning from someone that is better at something than you are.

A good competitor is:

Someone that knows that competition is good.

Someone that recognizes an opportunity to learn how to be better.

Someone that recognizes an opportunity to learn from a better competitor.

Someone that is a teacher.

Someone that does not become complacent.

Someone that knows that competing is not defeating, it is learning and teaching.

Someone that does not compete with only the purpose to defeat.

A good competitor is a successful person.

There are two groups of people, those that do and those that complain and try to take credit. Winners always come from the first group, there is less competition.

The successful competitor knows to exploit their strengths and avoid their weaknesses. Byorn Borg was one of the best tennis players of his time. He recognized his strength as being a base line player and his weakness was playing the net. When competing, his strategy was to force his opponent to also play from the base line, thus playing to his own strength.

COMPETITIVE GUIDELINES

1. *You compete against a person.* Know who you are competing against.
2. *Isolate important information.* Find and focus on the important information and filter out the unimportant.
3. *Be efficient* in analyzing information to avoid missing opportunities from delayed action or reaction.

BECOMING A COMPETITIVE TEACHER AND STUDENT

1. *Change your view.* Recognize that a good competitor is a good teacher, not just your opponent.
2. *Measure* your results against others.
3. *Form alliances* with former competitors who have shared goals, visions, interest and purpose.
4. *Stay centered on principles* and the positive avoiding the negative.
5. *Learn* from your opponents, better or not, there is always something to learn.

THE BOTTOM LINE

Single focused competitors are defeated from within. Internal competition defeats yourself, your allies and your teammates. A great and successful competitor is one that is both the student and the teacher. You must know and capitalize on your strengths and supplement and avoid your weakness.

A. Answer to previous chapter question.

"Come on in, and try not to ruin everything by being you."

As Good As It Gets

What Do You Want To Do Today?

CHAPTER NINE

Being Passionate and Enjoying What You Do

"Nothing great in the world has been accccomplished without passion."
— George Wilhelm

"I'd rather be a failure at something I enjoy than a success at something I hate."
— George Burns

WEBSTER'S
"Powerful emotion or appetite ... (to do what you) derive pleasure from."

MINE
"Being driven to do what you want and unable to imagine wanting to do anything else."

Being passionate about and enjoying what you do is important to achieving Personal Success.

Average people deliver average results. Being passionate about whatever you do can be the difference between the average or good and the exceptional or great. Passionate people believe in what they are doing and radiate enthusiasm that is infectious and attractive.

If you are unable to sleep well, you may not be enjoying what you do. If you find yourself laying awake at night and worrying, you may not be enjoying what you do. If you don't look forward to getting up in the morning, you may not be enjoying what you do.

Think about someone you know that is truly happy and you will most assuredly have found someone that enjoys what they do and do what they enjoy. Enjoying what you do is not mindless, passive, having no responsibilities, routine or unchallenging.

In his book *"Flow"*, Psychologist Mihaly Csikszentmihalyi (really) studied the psychology of enjoyment and the quality of life. According to his research, people have a need for complexity and challenge. Consider our leisure activities we choose for enjoyment like games, puzzles, paint ball combat, rock climbing, endurance bicycling, gardening, sports competition like golf, tennis, etc.

What does this mean? If your work does not present renewed challenges, opportunities to learn and grow with increasing complexities, you may not be enjoying what you do. You will be living the *"Been there, done that"* life. If you do not enjoy your work, it and you will become mediocre at best.

In his book Wisdom for a Young CEO, Douglas Barry asked 300 leading executives for advice. Mr. Barry states that the most important single thing he learned from their responses was simply to *"...follow your passion."*

In my experiences with successful people I have asked each one when they expect to retire. They all respond similarly, *"Retire and do what? I am already doing what I want to do."* One way they maintain their enthusiasm is that they don't do what they don't want to. By staying focused on whatever they enjoy, they remain mentally healthy and positive.

If they enjoy selling, they sell. They don't do billing, bookkeeping, paying bills, purchasing, etc. They have those tasks performed by professionals or employees.

In a restaurant, if they enjoy cooking, they cook. They don't clean, they don't pay bills, handle the money, seat people, take orders, etc. You get the idea.

It has been determined that those people that are happiest are also more closely aligned between what they enjoy and what they do.

Successful people keep focused on what they enjoy and don't get distracted or drawn into other things. It is all to easy to get side-tracked on other things that you don't enjoy or find tediously boring or emotionally draining. If you awake in the morning with things waiting for you that you don't enjoy, you won't look forward to doing what you do enjoy. This results in a long, tiring, unrewarding day and probably an unproductive day, week, month or year.

If you do not enjoy your work, then your family relationships and life will suffer. You will be miserable and your children will grow up and be miserable learning from you by example that being an adult means being miserable and having to do what you do not enjoy.

In his book *Masters of Success,* Dr. Ivan Misner, PH.D. identified seven traits common to successful people that have excelled in business, sports, arts and entertainment. One of the seven traits is *"...being passionate about what you're doing."*

If you have ever been to a meeting, play, seminar or any type of individually personal presentation or performance, thinking back, you may recognize that the value you received was directly proportional to the passion of the person presenting it. How can others be excited about your presentation and work if you aren't? Why should others become motivated if you are not? Highly intelligent or talented individuals can be informative but the passionate ones will get and keep your attention and leave you with something you will remember rather than probably already have forgotten before you leave.

Passion will separate you from the others that may know how to do the same thing, possibly even better, because your passion will permanently have your personal imprint, identity or slant on something that will make a connection with others that otherwise simply wouldn't happen.

It has been said, *"Most people prefer real to right."* and *"The world belongs to those that show up."* Your passion will communicate your sincerity, your enthusiasm, yourself; and people will pay attention, as long as you show up.

Lisa Whaley is a former IBM executive and author of the book *"Reclaiming My Soul from the Lost and Found"*. With a failing marriage and family life, after considering suicide, she left a 22 year career that others would consider successful, realizing she was not being fulfilled or enjoying what she did. For her, she was certainly not successful.

Ms. Whaley explains it as finding her personal SPA plan. *"STATE what you want to do: PLAN it so you can accomplish it: ACT on it."*

Passion is not found for a moment but rather is a lasting and driving force. You don't have to be the best. With passion you will achieve, sooner or later.

Kymberlee Weil with the firm *Mixed Grill* finds passion by being around people that inspire her and from whom she can learn from and be challenged by. Her belief, *"Follow your passion; it can change your life."*

If you never try, you'll be missing the job you were meant for.

BEING PASSIONATE AND ENJOYING WHAT YOU DO

1. *Successful people* follow their passion.

2. *Happy people* enjoy what they do and do what they enjoy.

3. *Passionate people* radiate enthusiasm to others, infect and elicit enthusiasm from others.

4. *If you do not enjoy your work,* at best it and you will be mediocre, living a *"Been there, done that"* life.

5. *To derive enjoyment* means to have complexity and challenges.

6. *Don't do what you don't enjoy.* Leave those tasks to others that do enjoy doing them.

7. *If you don't enjoy, value and appreciate what you do, why should others?* Don't be surprised if you are not noticed.

8. *Your passion* distinguishes and imprints your work above others and becomes memorable.

THE BOTTOM LINE

You will never be satisfied, happy or fulfilled without passion. If you don't enjoy what you do, how can you possibly be doing your best? You owe it to yourself. Quoting Ms. Weil "At the end of the day, you are the most important person in your life."

Q. What movie is the following line from?
"I'd rather have thirty minutes of wonderful
than a lifetime of nothing special."

CHAPTER TEN

Whatever You Do, Do It Well

"We are what we repeatedly do.
Excellence, then, is not an act, but a habit."

— Aristotle

WEBSTER'S
Well Done – *"Satisfactorily accomplished."*

MINE
"Done correctly, to the best of your ability, not just good enough."

"It is hard to fail but it is worse never to have tried to succeed."
—Theodore Roosevelt.

———❧———

"It is not the critic who counts; not the man who points out how the strong man stumbles, or where the doer of deeds could have done them better. The credit belongs to the man in the arena, whose face is marred by dust and sweat and blood; who strives valiantly ... who knows the great enthusiasms, the great devotions; who spends himself in a worthy cause; who at the best knows in the end the triumph of high achievement, and who at the worst, if he fails, at least fails while daring greatly, so that his place shall never be with those cold and timid souls who have never known neither victory nor defeat."

—Theodore Roosevelt

Successful people strive to do their very best and simply by having tried, they are successful.

The question isn't *"How much should you do?"* The question is *"How much can you do?"*

There are only two choices available to you: the first is to do all you can and the second is to do less. As motivational speaker Jim Rohn puts it, *"You can choose to be less than you were designed to be, or you can choose to be all you were designed to be."*

The successful person is not measured, for example, by how much they make. The amount is immaterial. The question is if they have done their best. Every person makes a choice.

Making $100,000 a year is failing to do your best if you are capable of making a million. Making $10,000 a year is a success as long as you have done your best. If you put forth all your intellectual and physical capabilities and capacities and have done your best, you are successful. If you have not, others will know it and, more importantly, you will know it. Unless you are one of those poor unfortunate souls lacking of any pride, you will never be able to feel good about yourself knowing you did not put forth your best effort.

You will earn the recognition you receive whether positive or negative. The choice is yours.

What keeps people from doing their best? Glad you asked!

Perfection. So many people feel that they must be perfect to be successful and their knowing that they cannot be perfect prevents them from trying to **do your best**.

Not accepting a challenge. If you are not willing to take a chance, to try, to find and press yourself to your limit, you will not **do your best**.

Comparison. If you compare yourself to others and are concerned or get discouraged because there might be someone that can or may do better than you, you will not be able to **do your best**.

Embarrassment. If you are afraid of being embarrassed, you will not try to **do your best**.

No sense of humor. The inability to laugh at yourself and acknowledge your limitations will keep you from trying to **do your best**.

Inability to forgive. By being able to forgive others mistakes you develop the ability to forgive yourself and in so doing you will **do your best**.

The solution for not really trying to do your best is to simply do your best. If you really cannot do any better, then you are doing your best and that is acceptable and you have achieved success.

When facing a disgruntled individual, an upset customer in business, someone relying on your efforts, work or performance, have you ever declared to someone, *"I am doing the best I can"?* What does this really communicate to the other person? This self-defines and declares the extent of your highest limits, talents, capabilities and abilities, the pinnacle of your potential and human achievement which has obviously failed to achieve or meet the expectations or demands of the task.

If this happens, ask yourself the following questions:

1. Would your supervisor or coworkers agree that you are doing your best?
2. Is your best effort or work independent of your mood, emotions or personal problems?
3. Did you put forth your best effort or work regardless of the requirements, load or demands?
4. Did you try as hard as you could and there was nothing else that you could have done better?
5. Did you keep a positive attitude when faced with adversity?
6. Did you keep from acting or looking like a loser?
7. Did you avoid making up excuses for your failures?
8. Did you avoid blaming others for your failures?
9. Be honest with yourself, did you really do your best?

If you answered "NO" to any of the preceding questions, you probably failed to **do your best**.

When consulting with a Company, I have often asked employees upon completion of an assigned task, *"Is this the best you can do?"* This question may have been mistakenly taken as disappointment with their work product. Sometimes this was true. However, more often it was for that individual to make a self-assessment as to their work product. If they took back their assignment, I took that to mean they had not done their best.

If or when they reply *"Yes it is"*, I accepted it as such and used it to make an assessment for assigning future projects and matching abilities with clients. This was my intention from the beginning. The individual that took the work back and returned their revised assignment later was viewed as someone that was simply only trying to do enough to get by.

When the work isn't good enough, I believe that there is always one of two truths.

The first: If you really have done poorly and not given your best, you have now closed the door on any future opportunity to deal with the other party by declaring you cannot do any better. You have clearly communicated to them that you are unable to rise to an acceptable level for their business or patronage. You may have lost an opportunity and most certainly have harmed a reputation (yours or the Company you work for).

The second: You really have tried your best and the demands, conditions or circumstances put upon you exceeded your abilities. It is better to acknowledge it, handle it in the best possible way and hope the other party is understanding and patient. They will probably recognize and appreciate your efforts and that you were presented with an unrealistic job. People understand that nobody is perfect.

But be honest. Most people can tell the difference between an excuse and an explanation, but they will always appreciate honesty.

The following is a perfect example that was a part of my life.

Looking to purchase a new pickup truck, I went to a dealership and was immediately ensnared by an awaiting salesman that had watched my every move since entering the parking lot like a vulture circling road kill. We took a truck for a test drive during which I, right from the beginning, asked several questions about available performance and safety features, sound systems, vehicle capacity, etc. The salesman did not know a single answer but assured me he could find out when we returned to the dealership. He made no effort to demonstrate or present any features or anything inside or outside the vehicle. The last half of the test drive was in almost total silence. We both obviously knew he had no answers.

Upon returning to the dealership, he invited me inside to discuss price and find the answers to my questions. I politely declined and left. I drove twenty miles down the road to another dealership for this manufacturer.

Approaching the front doors, I was once again captured by a salesman. This time, however, after introductions I asked him if he was familiar with the features of the truck that I was interested in. He assured me that he was. We found the model I wanted and he asked me to bring a favorite CD with us for the test drive. He inserted the CD and let it play while we drove, thus permitting a demonstration of the vehicles premium sound system with music he already knew I liked.

I asked the same questions that were asked of the first salesman, but this time the gentleman responded immediately with answers and even enthusiastically elaborated on interior and exterior features and details that I did not ask about (I am not mechanically inclined).

I purchased the truck.

The moral to this elaborate (if not wordy) story is that the first salesman obviously did not do his best. He had not even bothered to take the time to learn about his product. He knew it and I knew it. The amount of effort that he had put into his work was equivalent to his commission, zero.

The second salesman had put in his time and done his homework. His knowledge and enthusiasm for his product was evident, informational, infectious and appreciated, as well as rewarded with a commission.

You have probably experienced one or both of the same types of salesman in your past and, if so, what was the end result?

Don't chase the money. Make the money chase you.

Too many people use money as a measuring tool.

If your priority is the quality of your work, others will notice: your customers, clients, patients, fellow employees, subordinates, boss', piers, competitors.

Do a better job and the money will follow. That will distinguish you from the others. You will be sought out.

You can easily tell when dealing with an individual or Company that has money as the only priority. For example:

At a national automobile service Company, I purchased and had installed a six year car battery. After about six months, the battery failed. I returned and had a replacement installed. Shortly after, the news reported that the Company had sold and installed used batteries as new at several of their locations. Regardless of whether this was the action of greedy managers or corporate management, I have never dealt with this Company again.

An auto body repair company uses non-original parts instead of original manufacturers parts when parts are not readily visible or cannot be visibly distinguished. However, they charge for the more expensive original manufacturers parts.

An auto body repair company in preparing an estimate for the insurance company or customer, when the opportunity presents itself, the estimator physically alters damaged repairable part into damaged part that can only be replaced, at a greater cost and, of course, profit.

Especially in a business that deals with the public, every moment of business and every product or service you sell and/or deliver communicates whether you are doing the best you can or not and can have a permanent effect.

When you receive something you ordered and it is not correct, is this the best the Company can do?

When you engage the personal services of a professional and the service performed is poor and/or incorrect, is that the best they can do?

When you enter a fast food restaurant and are greeted by unoccupied tables with food, condiments or paper and plastic items on the tables, seats and floor that have been left behind and not cleaned by staff, (not discussing the person(s) table manners that left it that way) does the staff intend to represent that this is the best they can do?

At a restaurant, when you receive your food order and it is incorrect, burned, cold or sloppily slapped onto the plate, are they meaning to say that this is the best they can do?

The following is **what you don't want to hear** from someone who is failing to do their best. Two of the following examples are from real past experiences of mine.

Diner – *"Waiter, my escargot just crawled off the plate."*

Surgeon – *"You were in surgery for a splenectomy, right?"*

Surgeon – *"Are we performing a vasectomy or appendectomy?"*

Mechanic – *"Did I refill the brake fluid?"*

Mechanic – *"Did I tighten the lug nuts on the tires?"*

This isn't requiring perfection it is just intended to get you to honestly look at your efforts and understand that others will be also. Then ask yourself, ***"Is this the best you can do?"***

After an automobile accident many years ago, as part of my recovery program, I began Karate lessons. I sought the benefit of the stretching and strength exercises. One thing that the Sensei (teacher) always impressed upon his students as they exercised and practiced the Karate moves and techniques was, "You will benefit more by performing one move correctly rather than five incorrectly." It didn't have to be perfect, simply correct and the best you could do.

In business and life, successful people also practice what my Sensei taught. It is better to do one thing right than five things wrong. No number of incorrectly manufactured items or substandard services can measure up to one done correctly.

Young national coffee shop chain probably has the highest price for a cup of coffee in the country. Has grown, expanded and profited by preparing each and every cup of coffee they serve, the best that they can, not just "good enough" or "that will do". They purchase the best coffee beans and products without consideration of cutting costs. The company has repeatedly rated as one of the best companies to work for.

As an example, during the hurricane season of 2004 four hurricanes hit central Florida within three months causing billions of dollars in damage. Hurricane insurance has a deductible of usually at least 2% of your home value or coverage. So, for example, the deductible on a $200,000 home would be $4,000, which would be the expense of the homeowner.

A small home-building Company on the central west coast provides a quality of construction that is rare today and only builds thirty to forty homes a year. They are located in a predominantly retirement area and known for their exceptional construction. After the hurricanes, the owner of the Company toured the damage on every home that his Company had constructed. Thanks to the quality of their construction, the damage on their homes was minimal and cosmetic, unlike other homes in the same area. **The Company repaired the damage on every single one of the homes they had constructed over the years at no cost to the homeowners.**

I had a senior company executive once tell me that he believed there was a one to ten relationship with people. For every customer served that one person would tell ten others, bad or good. Therefore, do you want one person telling ten others how great you are or five people telling fifty others how terrible you are? He had built his career, business and personal life on that belief, and he had done very well.

If after the completion of a job you find yourself saying something like:

"That ought to hold it."
"That should work."
"That's good enough."
"That should be good."
"It's not right but that's what they wanted."
"If they wanted a better job, they should have paid more."
"No one will know."
"Nobody will know who did it."
"Nobody will be able to see that anyway."
"I'll be gone by the time anyone notices."
"That won't last but by that time, I'll be gone."
"That's not going to work but it isn't my problem."
"That's not right but it's none of my business."

Then you probably didn't do it correctly and **did not do your best.**

———⊰◦◦◦⊱———

Don't settle for 'good enough',
don't just be an exception, be exceptional.

WHATEVER YOU DO, DO IT WELL

1. *You do not have to be perfect,* just do your best.
2. *If you know better, do better.*
3. *Accepting Challenges* can help you find your limit.
4. *Be able to laugh at yourself.*
5. *Forgiveness* for others mistakes will teach you to forgive yourself.
6. *Always do your best.*

THE BOTTOM LINE

The saying, *"If it is worth doing, it's worth doing well"* is true. You should always try to do the best job you can at whatever you do. It will be recognized, appreciated and rewarded. Always doing your best will bring long term rewards that far exceed any short term perceived benefits of doing less. Doing your best represents one of the very fundamental definitions of success that separates you from the faineant and unsuccessful.

A. Answer to previous chapter question.
*"I'd rather have thirty minutes of wonderful
than a lifetime of nothing special."*
Steel Magnolias

Q. What movie is the following line from?
*"My darling girl, when are you going to understand
that 'Normal' (average) is not necessarily a virtue?
It rather denotes a lack of courage."*

Developing Your Team

CHAPTER ELEVEN

People Skills, Networking and Communication

"We don't accomplish anything in this world alone ... whatever happens is the result of the whole tapestry of one's life and all the weaving of individual threads from one to another that creates something."
— Supreme Court Justice, Sandra Day O'Connor

WEBSTER'S
"Providing occasion for conversation and conviviality."
"An informal system whereby persons having common interest assist each other."
"The exchange of ideas, messages, or information ..."

MINE
"Relating with others and forming positive relationships that promote future mutual beneficial support. Effectively expressing yourself while also actually listening to and understanding another and achieving a meeting of the minds."

Robert Stevenson, in his book *"How To Soar Like An Eagle In A World Full Of Turkeys"*, quotes an anonymous source, *"People don't care how much you know, until they know how much you care."* Mr. Stevenson states that *"From the initial contact I have with any person ... I want to get as much information as possible about them and I want to be able to remember (it) ..."*

A survey of 750 senior leaders by Chief Executive Magazine found that people skills were the most important driver resulting in success.

Like most things, you need to practice. After meeting someone, take a moment to think back and test yourself. Try to remember their complete name and any other details of the conversation. Name of their spouse, children, where they work, what they do, hobbies or interests, any other details or impressions of a personal nature. If you cannot even remember their name after a few minutes, then you most likely failed to really take an interest in them and they probably sensed that and will reciprocate in kind.

One executive described his technique in remembering people he meets. He asks questions about their job, family, interests, hobbies. As the conversation occurs and he listens to the answers, he paints a picture that incorporates the individual and everything he learns about them. On the foreheads of everyone in the picture he mentally places their names. The picture will include information about their job, spouse, children, interests and hobbies, vacations, achievements, etc. His mentally created picture that he visualizes and commits to memory will then later be recalled more easily in the future.

―――●●●――――

Recognize those relationships that are beneficial
from those that are detrimental.

Consulting for a Company Board of Directors, George, the dominant male director categorized me as a *"know it all"* and ignored my advice. The reason? Because my advice was based upon professional expertise, experience, company rules and even state laws. My relationship with George quickly became confrontational because his agenda was simply to do what he wanted, when he wanted to, without regards to rules, laws or even involving the other directors. He was further bolstered and supported by the Company manager, Phillip, who then both viewed my comments and advice as personal attacks since it conflicted with their own agendas.

After some time and building company problems, George was ultimately confronted by the stockholders with threatened litigation, both as a Director for gross negligence and for individual personal liability. George attempted to redirect blame to others: myself, other Directors, other Officers and Phillip, but all of his actions were well documented and upon realizing that he now stood alone, George responded with liberal vulgarity and even contempt. Even Phillip quickly distanced himself from George faster than you could say ENRON.

―――●●●――――

One cold dark winter night, the wind blew a young bird from his nest onto the frozen ground. As the snow began to cover him, the shivering little bird began to cry: chirp, chirp, chirp. Hearing his cry, a cow came over and looked at the cold, shivering little baby bird. The cow turned around and dumped a big, warm, steaming cow patty onto the bird. The little bird, now warmed, poked his little head up through the cow patty and again began chirping. Chirp, chirp, chirp. A passing coyote, hearing the chirping little bird, came over, lifted the baby bird up out of the warm cow patty and cleaned him off. Then, looking at the little bird, the coyote raised him up, opened his jaws, and dropped the little bird into his mouth, swallowing him whole in one gulp.

(Movie: My Name is Nobody)

The moral of these two stories is: People that dump on you aren't always trying to hurt you, and people that pick you up and clean you off aren't always trying to help. When you're up to your neck in crap, keep your mouth shut.

We were traveling with another couple and the husband, Steve was a friend and business associate that was the most people person I had ever known (he passed away). We stopped at a rest area on the interstate a few hundred miles from home where Steve entered the rest room a couple minutes before me while I stretched. As I was entering, he was leaving accompanied by an older man who was shaking his hand and telling Steve to please give him a call and to stay with him the next time he visited New York. After returning to the car, I asked Steve who that was. Steve responded with a story: That was John Williams. John has been a baker for seventeen years at the same bakery in New York City. He and his wife Sharon are returning to New York from Miami. They were down visiting and helping their daughter, Susan, while she was recovering from an appendectomy. Susan works for a travel agency and is doing fine and they need to get back to New York for the High School graduation of their other daughter,

Michelle. Michelle is going to attend New York University majoring in education to be a teacher. John hopes to retire within two years, at which time they plan to move to Florida. I said to Steve, "Only you would run into someone you know in an interstate rest area bathroom hundreds of miles away from home." Steve said, correcting me, "Oh, I didn't know him. I just met him. He was at the next urinal. But, I now have his name, address, telephone number and a place to stay whenever I get to New York." Remember, **this IS a true story!**

Your social skills will greatly determine your advancement or stagnation and will ensure a place in someone's memory which will tell you how well you performed or impressed them (see chapter on *IMPRESSIONS*). Have you ever met someone for the first time and then ran into them a short time later? If they remembered your name and some details of your previous conversation, then you must have favorably impressed them. If they did not remember, you failed.

As you are already aware, people seek out others of like interests. *"Birds of a feather flock together."* You will be able to identify and define the criteria that meet your personal or business standards and requirements just as others will make such determinations about you.

One exercise might be to sit down and make a list of the characteristics and descriptions of your closest friends or those that you do business with. Be brutally honest and include everything about them. How they deal with other people and their spouse or family, their temperament, honesty, trustworthiness, sensitivity, selflessness or selfishness, do they do what they say they will, how they handle pressure and conflict, morals, business conduct, type of business, their close associates and friends, responsiveness to your needs, any addictions like alcohol or drugs, etc.

Odds are when you complete this list you will see a great deal of yourself. Is this the person you want to be?

When it comes time to examining your life and seeing who you are, *"The best mirror you will ever have is the face of a friend."*

The key to improving or developing people skills and networking is communication. What is communication? It is not speaking to someone. It is not an endless narrative with a witness or witnesses present. It is not talking. Most people are speaking, waiting to speak or preparing to speak. Too many people are merely present during conversation, not to understand, but rather seeking the opportunity to reply.

———

"The biggest problem with communication,
is the illusion that it has taken place."
—George Bernard Shaw

———

Your ability to effectively communicate is second only to your appearance in others perception of you.

From studies on effective and ineffective resumes and cover letters from *Scripps Howard News Service,* they found that, *"even the smallest error in spelling or grammar can make the difference in the selection of one candidate over another."* They provided the following examples of rejected resumes:

"... I have been searching for a career change and have had littel luck in finding that 'Perfect Job.' " (It's "little", not "littel")

"I am ... Looking for a stationery office position." (It's "stationary" not "stationery")

"Bachelorette of Science in Business Administration" (Need I explain?)

"Fluent in writing, reading and specking French." But not using spell check.

"Preparing, exopditing and entrying benefits." But not proofreading.

"I hold a 149 IQ." But apparently not using it.

"Thank you for taking the time to overlook my resume." It was.

"I am a quick leaner, dependable and honest." I wonder how far he can lean?

Under the heading *"Dates of Employment"* – *"2004-2004"*

Cover letter. *"Attached is my resume. Thank you for your patients."* Since not applying in the medical field, should have been patience.

"I was instrumental in helping the company go through bankruptcy." This might be important in the airlines industry.

The *National Association of Colleges and Employers* asked employers what skill was most lacking in college job candidates. The number one answer was *"good communication skills."* **Communication skills was most often on top of the list of qualities sought after by employers.**

When a job candidate was asked to describe her strongest set of skills, her answer was, *"My computer illiteracy."* As reported by David Reese, President of Reflex Staffing, an applicant for an executive position stated during an interview that he was *"an experienced manager, defective with both entry level and seasoned professionals."*

Job recruiters have reported that, although college graduates are technically educated, they are often too shy to look them in the eye and shake their hands, fumbling their words and are inarticulate. Paul Baruda with a professional reference checking service puts it, *"... You can be the best _____ in the world, but if you can't tell people what you do or communicate it to your co-workers, what good is all of that knowledge?"*

The man who can think and does not know how
to express what he thinks
is at the same level of him who cannot think.

—Pericles

According to Leslie Bonner, coordinator of organizational development for Solutions 21, *"My experience is that (communication skills) is the Number 1 aspect employers look for."*

For positive communication, the other person must feel (whether true or not) that your meeting, conversation or discussion is important to you. Contemporary etiquette should be kept in mind. Just as President George W. Bush becomes greatly annoyed when, during a meeting or press conference, someone's cellular telephone rings, we should all be sensitive to our devices.

Consider the following guidelines:

Speak clearly and correctly. You can look great but if you can't put together more than a couple one or two syllable words and speak to be heard but not disruptive, you will not be taken seriously. Present thoughts clearly and concisely without *"You know?"* and *"Um."*

Make what you say substantive and interesting. People won't listen just because you're talking. Thoughtless, blurted responses go nowhere. You must have something meaningful to contribute. Always speak with intelligence. Try to present your thoughts in a manner that will be interesting.

Be language sensitive. Recognize your surroundings and people present and within earshot. You won't use the same language in mixed company at a cocktail party that you would with the old gang at the sports bar.

Sincerity. Be sincere about your thoughts, feelings and emotions. You will know when you are faking it and so will others.

Flattery will get you anywhere. If the other person thinks you are looking to them as an authority and helping you out, they will enjoy and want to speak with you and they will like you. Dr. Phillip McGraw writes in his book *Life Strategies: Doing What Works, Doing What Matters, "The number one need among all people is acceptance."*

Don't monopolize the conversation. A good conversation is a team participation. Don't try to keep others from talking by raising your voice to talk over them or begin talking or inter-rupting before someone else completes their sentence or point.

Be aware of yours and others emotions. Your emotions will influence your behavior. Manage your emotions to not let them overwhelm your ability to address the issues. You will want to recognize others emotions to empathize with them.

Compromise to fix a problem or resolve conflict. The desired outcome of a difference of opinion or confrontation is to reach a recognized mutually acceptable improvement or conclusion. Moderately compromising from your position when you still believe you are right to achieve resolution is alright as long as you still profit and it means everybody wins.

Be open to change and a difference of opinion. Only a stubborn person will hold their position even when shown to be wrong. Be open to different views and new ideas.

Asking questions. Usually the most popular and best conver-sationalists are people that are able to get others to talk about themselves.

Listen. Many people are trying to think about what they are going to say next and miss what the other person is saying. Be sure to really listen to the other person. If you are focused only on listening for a break in their speaking, you probably aren't listen-ing. Don't let your eyes wander while they are talking. This tells the other person that you aren't interested in what they are say-ing and are looking for somewhere to move on to. As stated by Robert Stevenson in his book *How To Soar Like An Eagle In A*

World Full of Turkeys, "... There is a simple rule applied to be a successful communicator ... Listen twice as much as you speak."

Be considerate. Turn off your beeper or cellular phone and let the other person know that they are important to you.

Be flexible. Learn to adapt quickly to changing dynamics, people, subjects and conversation and go with the flow.

Be prepared. You at least should have some general thoughts about whatever the subject is. For example, if you are going to a wine tasting event and know nothing about wines, do some quick advance preparation.

Respect. Be respectful of others and their views whether you like or agree with them or not. Others around you will then like and respect you. You will be successful. If they think you're a disrespectful know-it-all schmuck, you have failed.

Follow up. If you get some worthwhile information or lead be sure to follow up with a telephone call to that person or a personal note. That personal touch will be well remembered.

As will always be the case, we live in a time of unprecedented technology that provides if not encourages less personal contact. The internet, computer answering systems, facsimile machines, telephones and cellular telephones, personal data assistants, etc. This makes it easier to become less attentive to quality, service and professionalism. If you do not return a telephone call from someone you have not met and they think that you are ignoring them and being unresponsive, so what? Maybe you are rude to them on the telephone. They were just a faceless person whose name you did not know on the telephone. Building and making human personal contact will distinguish you above others and will be remembered and rewarded.

Communication also incorporates nonverbal skills. For example, when meeting someone, especially for the first time, if you are wearing sun glasses and continue to wear them, you will be creating a barrier between yourself and the other person. By eliminating eye contact, you depersonalize the social moment and keep the other person at an impersonal distance and possibly even communicate unintended intimidation. This is alright if that is your intent, however, if you want to make a friendly personal impression, remove the sun glasses.

Always be sensitive to an individual's personal space. Every individual has a personal space that establishes their comfort zone or barrier. If you violate that space, they will move away from you to increase the distance between you. This is especially true with the opposite sex. Be aware of this and do not adjust to move closer.

According to Robert Sommer, psychologist at the University of California and author of the book *"Personal Space"*, *"The violation of personal space increases tension levels enormously."* According to Sommer, Americans require a comfort zone of 6 to 8 square feet around them, and a social distance of 4 feet or greater for conversing with acquaintances. A violation of this space results in an "in your face" feeling. As one executive states, *"If someone's a close-talker, it makes me instantly not like them."*

Sommer's study established that women have a smaller comfort zone than men and Americans have a larger comfort zone than Asians. Physical contact, other than an initial hand shake, should be avoided when first meeting.

Successful people work to maintain that personal touch. In business and personal relationships they make the extra effort to meet people even when they don't particularly need to, especially in the beginning. They want the other person to recognize them by name and face so they can associate with future contacts.

By networking with others, you will benefit by their work and progress just as they will yours. Therefore, by working with your selected or created network of like or complimentary interests, you would expect to get where you want to much faster.

According to studies, 60% to 90% of jobs are found as a result of networking. To build and establish a network, consider the following suggestions.

Identify your target. Identify the people, groups, trade shows, conferences, organizations or company's that you wish to network and build relationships with. For business, this will include potential networked business partners or clients. Personally this may be individuals of similar interests or hobbies, someone you may wish to pursue a relationship with, someone that can help solve some personal problem, etc.

Identify contacts. You probably already have established contacts through family and relatives, friends, neighbors, satisfied business customers. Use those contacts to create avenues of introduction.

Opportunities. Don't miss opportunities to initiate and meet people unexpectedly by chance. This could be on an airplane, standing in line at the movies, waiting for a table at a restaurant, etc. Be prepared for those opportunities. Be sensitive of your appearance and language. Your actions, appearance, behavior and language during what you may think is a private moment could very well not be and end up costing you a valuable opportunity.

Strategy and preparation. Not having a networking strategy is like picking stock investments by throwing darts at the Wall Street Journal. Prepare in advance a ten second introduction of who you are and/or what you do. Then have a follow up thirty second presentation of yourself or your business. Above all be sure to be genuine, honest and authentic, it will show.

Become a friend. An inviting smile will welcome your greeting and make you more approachable. Develop a firm handshake. Strong enough for a man but gentle enough for a woman (sorry). Facial expressions and eye contact will communicate your interest in the other person. Take note of the color of the persons eyes, unique facial expressions or physical characteristics. Listen carefully to their name, and do whatever it takes to commit it to memory.

Associate with them. Look them over for anything that would provide a recognizable common ground. A golf tie or tie clip, an associative piece of jewelry that might represent or symbolize a hobby, sport or group membership, like a club pin or ring. Familiarize yourself with brand and product names. For example, if a person is wearing *Maui Jim* sunglasses, you know they spent more for high quality lens sun glasses as opposed to an inexpensive brand and they will appreciate that you recognized that.

Listen. Really listen to what they have to say and their stories. Learn as much as you can through appropriate questions. Do not let your eyes wander around while they are talking. If you see their eyes wandering while you are talking, move on. You have lost their interest.

Business cards. Ask for their business card. Treat their card with respect and interest. When you get a moment, make notes from your conversation on the card so you won't forget. If you promised to contact them with some information, make sure you note it for later action. Normally, don't offer your business card until it is requested, unless you read the specific situation otherwise.

Work on quality contacts, not quantity. You and others can quickly tell if someone is really interested in establishing a relationship or just wanting to make as many contacts as possible and pass out and collect business cards. Focusing on the quality of the connection will be rewarded by earning the other persons respect and trust.

Don't come across pushy or desperate. Avoid coming on to desperate, strong or pushy. It will turn people off.

Referrals. Make referrals of people within your network that may solve someone's problem or need. This will make you a problem solver, establish your credibility and probably provide you return referrals.

Keep records. As your network is established, builds, grows and evolves, keep records and update information that you gather and learn through each experience. It always makes a memorable impression when you know a spouses name, the names of their children, someone's birthday, anniversary, important family events like vacations, graduations, etc.

Follow up. After you first meet a person, it is not the end but only the beginning.

Personal notes. According to the U.S. Postal Service, only 4% of mail is personal. A personal note will put you in front of the other 96%. Sending a personal note addressing something you talked about is a good idea shortly after first meeting them. If you receive a referral from them, send a personal note as a thank you. If you hear or read in the newspaper something about them or their company, send them a note, especially if the news is of a personal accomplishment or family nature.

Coffee, tea or lunch. After some time or if you have not heard from them in a while, call and invite them to lunch or meet for a cup of coffee. This should be a social meeting and not a business pitch.

Get them involved. Invite them to play a round of golf, game of tennis or go to a sporting event, anything. Naturally include some of your existing networked contacts or maybe some other new ones.

Stay in touch. People have short memories. Find a reason to make frequent contact with them, like monthly or bimonthly depending on the relationship.

Networking is not a moment in time but a process and pursuit over time and requires work and patience.

Dr. Phillip McGraw in his book *Life Strategies: Doing What Works, Doing What Matters* writes that *"The world couldn't care less about thoughts without action. People don't care about your intentions. ... You must commit to measuring yourself and everyone else on the basis of outcomes."*

I have always firmly believed that *Actions Speak Louder Than Words.* You should measure yourself and your relationships based upon actions and outcomes not upon promises, thoughts or intentions.

When you are part of a relationship, social group, network, etc., you will know where the strengths and weaknesses are within that group by the actions and outcomes with and by each individual. Others will know the strength of their relationship with you by your actions, not your good intentions.

Don't make promises you can't keep.
Don't make commitments you won't follow through with.
Don't say something if you are not sincere.
Don't break your word.

PEOPLE SKILLS

1. *Speak clearly,* correctly and to be heard.
2. *Be interesting,* intelligent and meaningful.
3. *Use appropriate language* and grammar.
4. *Be sincere and honest.*
5. *Be flattering* when appropriate.
6. *Don't monopolize the conversation.*
7. *Be aware and sensitive* to your emotions and the emotions of others.
8. *Be willing to compromise* as long as you still achieve your goal and others also feel successful.
9. *Be open to change* and different opinions.
10. *Ask questions.* Get them talking about themselves.
11. *Listen, really listen* to what others have to say.
12. *Be flexible* and react to changing circumstances.
13. *Prepare in advance* as much as possible.
14. *Always respect the other person* even when you don't agree.
15. *Follow up* with personal contact.

NETWORKING

1. *Identify your target* people, group, etc.
2. *Identify existing contacts.* Family, relatives, friends, good business relations.
3. *Always be open for an opportunity.*
4. *Have a pre-prepared strategy,* introduction and presentation.
5. *Become a friend* to all.
6. *Find something associative* with others.
7. *Listen to what they have to say* and what is important to them. It will be important to you.
8. *Always have business cards* at the ready.
9. *Work for quality contacts* not quantity.
10. *Don't be pushy* or seem desperate.
11. *Make referrals* to receive referrals.
12. *Keep informational records.*
13. *Follow up* with personal notes, social meetings and interactive activities.
14. *Actions speak louder than words.* Measure yourself and others based on actions and outcomes, not promises, good intentions or claims.

COMMUNICATION

1. Written
    A. Use Spell Check
    B. Proofread
    C. Check Grammar
2. *Practice with conversations.*
3. *Be articulate and decisive.*
4. *Become grammatically correct.*
5. *Ask intelligent questions.*
6. *Have intelligent answers.*
7. *Everyone you meet needs attention, give it to them.*
8. *Be approachable.*
9. *Listen.* Don't tune others out.
10. *Be considerate.* Turn off electronic communications.

THE BOTTOM LINE

People Skills, Networking and Communication takes work, practice and a continued effort. The degree of success will be directly related to the amount of effort invested and personal skills achieved. The person with the best People Skills is the one that is truly interested in or develops an interest in others. How well you communicate with others will be an asset or a liability, whichever you make it, there is no other choice. Developing a productive and beneficial network means seeking out those of like-kind characteristics and ethics. Associate yourself with those that hold your same values and disassociate yourself with those that do not. Sincerity and being yourself is important. Don't kid yourself, you and others will recognize a false pretense disappointing both yourself and them.

A. Answer to previous chapter question.
"My darling girl, when are you going to understand
that 'Normal' (average) is not necessarily a virtue?
It rather denotes a lack of courage."
Practical Magic

Q. What movie is the following line from?
"In this world ... You must be oh so smart
or oh so pleasant. Well for years I was smart.
I recommend pleasant."

CHAPTER TWELVE

Professional Advisors

"Let others make your decisions and you will get what they deserve."
— Mark C. Middleton

WEBSTER'S
*"Possessing great skill or experience in a field
or activity and who offers advice."*

MINE
*"Individual with specialized training, experience and expertise that
after reviewing and considering all the facts, provides their advice
in order for you to make a decision."*

All professional advisors are exactly that, advisors. You and you alone are the decision maker. When seeking advice from professionals, in many cases, we have all been somewhat conditioned and trained to accept their advice and "decisions" as being the final answer.

When was the last time you:

> Challenged or even questioned your doctor or dentist about your medication, tests, procedures or prescribed medical treatment?

> Questioned your income tax professional about specific details or treatment of income or deductions on your income tax return instead of just signing it where they tell you?

> Questioned your investment advisor about which investments they recommend and why for your specific investment criteria, family, age, retirement, etc., especially when your investments are not performing?

> Asked your insurance agent about specific coverage and limits before you have a need for a claim?

> Question your attorney about a litigation issue, strategy, contract, will or trust?

Most of us have been trained over the years to simply accept their advice, sometimes without question, sign where indicated, without understanding or even reading, and accepting their decisions to be correct and right for you and your life.

I think I can safely say that in most cases, professional advisors spend a very limited amount of time reviewing your specific individual situation and yet you permit them to make decisions for you that will affect the rest of your life and many times are a result of their simply pigeonholing or diagnosing you based upon a limited set of criteria and *"selling"* you a packaged service or plan instead of a tailored service or plan. That packaged service or plan is usually the same thing they have sold to many others.

You might consider the following suggestions when looking for and interviewing a professional advisor.

Make inquiries. Ask for referrals from family, friends, associates and other professionals. Look particularly for those that are recommended based upon positive and favorable experiences. Their reputation and integrity is important. To me this rates higher than, he's my neighbor, she's in the (insert name here) club with me, he's my in-law, etc.

Interview. Always remember, advisors work for you. They will not make any money if you do not retain their services. They are not interviewing you, you are interviewing them.

Compatibility and impression. Your advisor must be compatible with your needs. You wouldn't retain a brain surgeon to diagnose and treat a cold. See what impression they make. As a security expert once advised me, *"No matter how good or secure the situation seems, if for any reason you have a bad feeling about the person, even if you don't know why, go with that feeling and leave. Find someone else. Trust your instincts."*

Personal interest. The professional should take time to understand your specific situation. Their advice should address your desired and expected results and needs. Based upon their experience and expertise, they should present issues that you have not thought of and not simply address only those you have. They should not practice a *"One size fits all"* approach, but take time to recognize, identify and investigate all issues related to you.

Qualifications. Make sure your prospective advisor is qualified. Many accreditation's or designations are recognizable. For example, we all know that the letters CPA after a name stands for Certified Public Accountant and is only awarded after a specified achievement of formal education, substantial testing and apprenticed work experience, with required continuing education. However, there are many accreditation's that are received after simply attending a short seminar or presentation or submitting a small fee, that might be used as an inference or for an impression of something more than what it really is. Inquire of any presented accreditation's or designations that you do not recognize and ask for a description of how such designation was received being specific as to what was required to be accomplished for the right to such usage.

Know who you are hiring. You expect the work to be performed by the person you hire. If that professional is assigning your job to others and only supervising them (at least you hope), you should know this and probably interview those others also and make sure you are comfortable with this structure. More professional services retained locally are sub-contracted to foreign '*professionals*' without your knowledge.

Understand how and how much compensated. You are not asking them how much their salary is, amount of any performance bonus or benefits package, but if they are making a commission based upon their services, you should know this. If they are charging strictly a flat fee, hourly fee or a percentage based upon results, whatever. Your costs and their compensation structure should be disclosed up front.

Responsiveness and communication. The advisor must be responsive to you. Do they return phone calls timely? Do they answer your questions completely? Do they keep you informed about their actions based upon your decisions and directions? Do they communicate with you or delegate this to a subordinate?

Their work load and resources. There are excellent advisors that simply spread themselves too thin resulting in the sacrifice of quality services or needed resources to service the client/patient. This will usually be detected in responsiveness.

Results or performance. Their services should result in achieving your goals even if that is simply to provide their best possible service and effort.

The most feared and empowered client or patient is the one that is the most informed. To the extent possible, research your issues prior to meeting with your professional advisor. When possible and/or appropriate, provide the advisor with an agenda in advance of the meeting and be as clear, precise, detailed, specific and brief as possible. This will put them on notice that you are prepared and informed and they will spend more time in preparation for your meeting and have more information available and ready at no expense to you.

If all this creates a problem for your advisor or makes them uncomfortable, you have probably found one that is only interested in you for their own profit and/or to the extent that it furthers their own convenience, benefit, interests or is simply too busy. Find a different advisor.

All professional advisors provide a service and are in PRACTICE to be:

1. Proficient in their field of expertise.
2. Responsive to your individual situation.
3. Accountable for their actions and end results.
4. Communicative with you.
5. Totally committed.
6. Involved personally.
7. Capable to commit needed and necessary time and resources.
8. Experienced for your situation.

That's why they call it a **PRACTICE** instead of a job.

The character of your advisor should be compatible with your character.

> *An insurance agent sets up a company retirement plan for a small Corporation and overstates the funding. Upon the accountants' notification, the insurance agents' response is, "Since the IRS knows only what we report to them, they will never find out."*

My professional opinion/advice would be that you shouldn't do business with this Agency. You want someone that will stand behind their good advice as opposed to solving problems with bad advice. They most assuredly will not accept responsibility when bad advice goes bad.

According to *Healthgrades, Patient Safety In American Hospitals, July 2004*, medical errors kill 195,000 Americans every year.

According to the *Institute of Medicine, To Err is Human: Building a Safer Health System, November 1999*, medical errors cost the economy up to $29 billion every year. This is quantified in dollars only not in pain, suffering and death.

From my own personal experience, after waiting about twenty minutes in an examination room for the Doctor, he came in and spent forty seconds (yes seconds) with me. They conveniently had a wall mounted clock in the room. I got dressed, went to the receptionist behind the counter, received my prescription and paid seventy five dollars.

Dr. Paul Yoon with the Center for Disease Control's (CDC) Family History Initiative states that *"Doctors average less than 2.5 minutes discussing family history and rarely include a family tree in a patient's file."* Why is this important? Genomics is the study of the entire set of human genes. Dr Muin Khoury, director of the Office of Genomics and Disease Prevention at the CDC, states that you have 10,000 to 15,000 genes, which is half of your total, in common with your biological parents, brothers and sisters. This is more than available in any lab test. Knowing family history will tailor medical tests and treatment programs making them specific for you.

How does this help? As an example, about 30% of people that would take a daily aspirin are resistant to the anti-clotting benefits. Doctors routinely prescribe this for prevention of a heart attack. A family history could reveal this genetic resistance and direct treatment to another more tailored anti-clotting medication.

Pharmacogenomics combines modern genetic research with pharmaceuticals. People react differently to medications based upon their levels of different enzymes that affect their absorption rate of medications. A person that quickly breaks down the medication needs a larger dose or more frequent dose than one who breaks down the medication less rapidly who could be poisoned by a larger or more frequent dose.

The difference in enzymes is based upon different types of genes which vary between ethnic groups.

This means that one medication appropriate for a Caucasian would be ineffective or less effective for an African American. ACE-inhibitors, on average, are ineffective for treating heart failure in African Americans, whereas, they are an effective standard treatment in other ethnic groups.

Eskimos metabolize the medication, isoniazid, much faster than the general population because they have a variant form of a liver enzyme. This makes this part of the treatment for tuberculosis ineffective for Eskimos

According to Dr. Stephen Liggett, professor of medicine at the University of Cincinnati, doctors traditionally prescribe the same treatment program for all patients for a specific health problem. *"If one medication fails, which happens about 50% of the time, they change doses or try another drug. Trial and error remains standard practice."*

Why? Because of expediency, economics and outdated training.

As Dr. Liggett notes, if you have asthma that would mean several years of suffering. With congestive heart failure, this can be fatal.

As recommended by Dr. Cathy McCarty, director of the Personalized Medicine Research Center at Marshfield Clinic, *"Personalized Medicine advances genomics"* and, according to Dr. Khoury, *"The ultimate genomic test is available now, a family history."*

Find a medical professional that understands these sciences and takes the time to practice Personalized Medicine instead of Production Medicine.

Successful people may have the financial resources to seek out such medical professionals but we should all be demanding it and avoid those professionals that simply categorize everyone into their stale, outdated, preconceived treatment programs.

According to Scott Herpich, attorney with Lathrop & Gace, LC, *"It's a red flag if your adviser has something tangible to gain if you, in fact, follow their guidance. Also, get advice in writing, particularly if there is an element of risk involved. Advisers tend to be a lot less glib when they have to commit their words to paper. In their own self-interest, they have to spell out downsides more clearly."*

Annuities pay a commission to those selling them of around 5% to 7% but can be as much as 13%. This commission is paid out of the amount that you invest or purchase. Therefore, a $100,000 annuity purchased can pay an average of $7,000 in commission to the person or Company selling the annuity which results in your beginning investment balance of $93,000. It will take your account some time to recover that commission.

As Mr. Herpich stated, you should be very suspect of the advice when your investment advisor has a financial stake in your decision, and always remember, it is your decision. In addition, if that personal stake was not disclosed up front without probing questions from you, find another advisor.

If any advisor has a vested interest (financial or otherwise) in the decision you make based upon their advice, then their advice is suspect as to:

Credibility

Objectivity

Judgment

Independence

Value

You may be best served by using advisors that are fee based only. Meaning, they simply charge you for their time and are in no other way compensated.

As has been said, *"Good consultants tell people what they need to know, not what they want to hear."* I would also add to that *"Good consultants answer the questions that you did not think or know to ask."*

I would like to impress on all who read this, the experienced and the naive, the truth about our judicial system, based upon years of personal experience working with attorneys, discussions with attorneys and judges, pier experiences and observations:

The judicial system is not based upon guilt or innocence.
The judicial system is not based upon right or wrong.
The judicial system is not based upon retribution.
The judicial system is not based upon punishing the guilty, protecting the victimized innocent or compensating those damaged.

The judicial system is an arena in which you win or lose, period.

Nancy Grace is the author of the book *"Objection."* During her career as a prosecutor, she won almost 100 convictions with no losses. In her book she characterizes the defense attorney as ethically deficient and akin to a con artist trained *"... to obscure the truth from the jury."*

Pop quiz – Question: What is the highest court in the country?
        Answer: The court of public opinion.

Often legal actions taken are a result of public opinion or pressure.

A large international business account manager makes a transaction that loses money for a client. In order to save face and redirect blame, (certainly he could not possibly be responsible), he sues the small company that simply processed the transaction. Since the large company had a staff of attorney's, the small company was put out of business. Litigation still pending and bankruptcy for small company and owners is possible. Although the small company did no wrong, they cannot mount a defense against the larger company. The larger company won not because they were right but simply because they could afford to win.

When selecting your Professional Advisors, certainly choose those that you are comfortable with, have taken the necessary time to understand and consider your situation and goals and feel will truly provide advice that is with your best interest in mind.

Always remember that you and only you must live with the decisions you make based upon the advice you receive and rely on for the rest of your life. You must choose wisely.

CHOOSING A PROFESSIONAL ADVISOR

1. *Make inquiries* and get referrals.
2. *Interview* and remember, you are interviewing them.
3. *Make sure they are compatible with you* and that you have a good feeling about and impression with them.
4. *They should take a personal interest* in your situation and not have a "one size fits all" approach.
5. *Make sure they are qualified* to address your situation.
6. *Know who you are hiring* to do the work. If they are using others, find out up front.
7. *Know how they are to be compensated* by you and any others: how it affects your account and what is expected from you.
8. *Advisor's should communicate* with and be responsible to you.
9. *Advisor should have sufficient time and resources* to handle your situation.
10. *Their advice or work should achieve your desired results.*
11. *If advisor is uncomfortable with your requirements, find a new advisor.*
12. *Make sure your professional advisor adheres to their PRACTICE.*

THE BOTTOM LINE

Professional advisors are not decision makers, you are. Avoid using production professionals. You should seek out advisors that have the proper training, experience, qualifications and credentials, and can personally take whatever time is needed to tailor and provide you the best possible advice for your specific issue that is in your best interest. You want advisors in PRACTICE, not just doing a job or delegating it to someone else. You should not use a professional advisor that has a personal stake in your decision, their advice will be suspect. What actions you take or don't take based upon their advice is your decision, not theirs. It is your life, not theirs.

A. Answer to previous chapter question.
"In this world ... You must be oh so smart
or oh so pleasant. Well for years I was smart.
I recommend pleasant."
Harvey

Q. What movie is the following line from?
"Don't make my mistake, kid.
Don't follow orders your whole life.
Think for yourself."

CHAPTER THIRTEEN

Motivating Others

*"The art of getting someone else to do something you
want done because he wants to do it."*

— Dwight D. Eisenhower

WEBSTER'S

(Training) "To coach in or accustom to a mode of behavior or performance."

MINE

*"To move and/or stimulate others to take actions because
they want to that will be for your benefit."*

This is not just about motivating, training or teaching employees or
others. This is not just about dealing with people that you are related to, in
charge of, or that you pay. This is different from People Skills or
Networking. This is about getting others not only to do what you want,
but to do what you want better and because they want to and not have to.

To me, this is related to but different from people skills or networking. This is about dealing with others, not just for business,

profit or employment but also those that can have an impact on your life and your quality of life.

Through all aspects of life there are always others that have the ability to make your life better, more comfortable, less stressful, more fulfilled, easier or help expedite the achievement of your goals and resolve problems. You will always have three choices when dealing with others:

Negative Motivation – Motivate others to work against you and be problematic. When you antagonize someone, be insulting, disrespectful, condescending or make them angry, they will be motivated to not offer any assistance at the least and more likely even create problems and delays at the most.

Unmotivated – When you impress someone to total indifference towards you. They are not interested in and don't care about you.

Positive Motivation – When someone takes a personal interest in you or your problem and they want to help you.

Speaking in generalities, the sad reality is that a majority of people are employed in an unrecognized, thankless, underpaid, under appreciated, mundane, boring, unexciting, repetitive, routine dead-end job, often reporting to and/or working with people, they have little in common with, don't like or even make their lives miserable for at least one-third of their day, while they think or daydream of how things could have, should have or would have been different only if ..., whatever! (Not only a long sentence but also very depressing.)

Why is this noteworthy? Because those are the same people that will respond the most to a little personal attention or recognition and become positively motivated.

I came to this realization of motivating others first through self-analysis as to why I myself was more motivated to provide additional work and attention at no additional charge to some clients and not for others. Not that I ever short changed any client, but there were some clients I provided extra for because I knew they would recognize and appreciate it and I didn't want to disappoint them. What did they do to distinguish themselves differently and create this drive within myself?

These were clients that were always thankful for my time, complimentary and appreciative towards my work product or advice, sent personal notes or thank you cards, forwarded noteworthy information from newspapers, magazines or publications they thought I would be interested in, business or personal. Through conversations, they knew of my personal interests and hobbies and exploited that knowledge. I wanted to do better for them. They made me want to do better.

The second phase of this motivating others realization was from being with and watching successful people and how they had motivated or trained others around them; employees, bosses, the bank tellers, restaurant servers, etc. Whenever they interacted with someone they had already met or dealt with, that person was more attentive and responsive. The successful person would go out of their way to meet someone they had not.

As noted by Dr. Phillip McGraw in his book *Life Strategies: Doing What Works, Doing What Matters,* "*We teach people how to treat us.*"

Armed with and applying this discovery, I had the following simple experience:

> *I often eat breakfast at McDonalds. The 'cook' probably assembles 300 Egg McMuffin's an hour. Not meaning to be critical, but often in their haste the alignment of the egg, Canadian bacon and cheese is not only askew to each other but also to the muffin. In addition, I*

prefer a muffin with no blackening around the edge. The same crew usually works when I am there. One time when my Egg McMuffin came out correctly, I made a point of talking to the shift manager who also called the "cook' over and complimented the crew on the sandwich describing exactly why I liked it. I believe this provided recognition, appreciation and acknowledgment, especially in front of their boss. They realized that someone was recognizing their personal performance. My Egg McMuffin's have always come out perfect from then on.

My vet Vicki provides outstanding medical care for by Schnauzers (dogs). After performing minor surgery on two of them, I sent a personal thank you letter acknowledging and thanking her for the superior care she showed my animals in the past. Once again, some surgery was necessary and I made an appointment. Vicki extended her appreciation for the letter, performed the needed surgery and also provided some additional medical services at no additional charge. Every annual checkup now includes a thorough exam. My vet has always provided a superior service, but from then on there was notice-ably more time spent with the annual exam and other services.

During my career as a Certified Public Accountant I had to do much research related to tax planning in light of changing tax laws, tax court decisions, tax law cases, investment strategies, trust strategies and so on. During the last few active years of my career, I had attorney's, other accountants, real estate brokers, financial consultants, stock brokers, business executives and other professionals that would call and provide information and copy me on cases, strategies and planning encountered in their practices'. Much of my research and homework was being done for me. Okay, this is more related to networking, however, still is a good example of getting others to do some of my work and making my life easier through training.

You will find people throughout your travels that will respond positively to a simple compliment, acknowledgment of their work, notice of effort, their belief that you look to them as the expert, sympathy for workload, etc.

Food services (waiters, hosts, cleaning, kitchen), sales people, mechanics, cleaners, delivery, transportation, government workers (Federal, State, County, City), professionals, personal services, medical, Post Office, Internal Revenue Service, Social Security Administration, an endless list.

> *Steve, a friend of mine was building his own house. The County approval and permitting process to the inexperienced is daunting. During his first visit to the permitting office Steve went out of his way to be pleasant, complimentary and sympathetic to the overworked and overburdened employee expressing his amazement for her ability to manage the daily demands. She responded with the expeditious computer accessing (which Steve was suppose to do himself) and filing of necessary forms. Every time Steve went to that office again, she was attentive to personally address his needs and resolve any problems.*

The restaurant host/hostess that gets you seated faster and at a better table or the waiter/waitress that processes your order faster or provides extra services. The salesman that makes sure you receive the best price for the best product. Maybe the taxi driver that directs you to the best local restaurants or the Flight Attendants that provide extra drinks and snacks. The hotel concierge that acquires show tickets to sold out shows. The tour services personnel that direct you where and where not to go and when.

Probably none of these will further your career, so this is not really a networking point. However, they all can improve your life or the quality of your life.

Your social skills will be measured by how successful you are in winning or earning their attention, respect and measure how much they want to help you. For example, asking permission versus giving orders:

"Could I possibly get some more of that absolutely wonderful bread you baked?"

Will probably be received much more positively than:

"Get me some more bread." Or even,

"Get me some more bread, please." You are still giving an order.

Because as much as others can help you if they want to, if alienated or moved to negative motivation, they can go out of their way to be problematic.

Fast food service drive through customer is loud, abusive and sarcastic. The cook spits on his burger before wrapping and putting it in the bag to be handed through the window to the customer.

In interviews, fast food workers admitted to gathering bird droppings to mix into food prepared for customers that they found annoying or irritating.

A rude restaurant customer receives the bread that has cooled down instead of the fresh, warm bread right out of the oven. In addition, salad is made from lettuce with browned edges instead of the fresher lettuce.

Consider the following techniques that you might apply in a work related or any other common life situation:

Watch the little things. Say *"Good morning." "Thank you."* Often it is the little things that mean the most.

Listen to what they have to say. Really listen. Alienation of others can begin when they don't think you are listening.

Do as you say. If you expect people to only take a one hour lunch, you only take a one hour lunch. Others notice if you have double standards.

Do what you say. If you expect others to stay true to their word, you must be true to your word. Keep promises and commitments

.

Ask for their advice. Asking for advice from someone says that you value their opinion and also if they are able to assist you, they will work harder.

Be approachable and available. There are always times when you are needed and/or should be involved. If you do not make yourself available, you will soon not be sought.

Keep them informed. If they are important then they should be kept informed. You will benefit and they will continue to feel a part.

Praise or thank them for their work. Let them know they make a difference.

Tell their boss what a good job they did. Everyone appreciates it when there is something good to say. Unfortunately, usually there is only something said when there is a problem.

Handle reprimands and negative actions tactfully and constructively. Create a learning process, not to punish, embarrass, demean, hurt or create an enemy.

Avoid being dictatorial. Define goals, provide input and guidance and let others do their job.

Acknowledge your own errors. No one is perfect. Don't blame others. You won't regret it and others will think you a bigger person.

Help others build on their strengths and be successful. The success of others will be yours also.

Reward achievements. Success and achievements should be recognized and rewarded to whatever extent possible.

Balance responsibility, authority and capability, as an employer or supervisor. The disparity of any one will result in failure.

Motivating others does not mean pushing or driving them. You want to help and encourage others to live up to their potential, not your expectations. This will be mutually beneficial for them and you, but always remember that it is their life and their choice, not yours.

The parents of a two year old are adamant that their son grows up to be an athlete, all of his clothes have sports team logos and toys all relate to sports activities. They even have him on an exercise regimen. They have stated that if he does not become a professional athlete, they will be greatly disappointed in him.

MOTIVATING OTHERS

1. *Pay attention to details.* It's the small things that count.
2. *Listen to what others have to say.* You may actually not know everything.
3. *Don't expect others to do what you don't or won't.*
4. *Do what you say you will or won't.* Don't go back on your word.
5. *Ask advice.* Others may have ideas that you did not think of.
6. *Be available when you are needed.* If something or someone fails because you could not be reached, then you have failed them.
7. *Keep others in the loop.* Those involved should be kept involved or you will find yourself alone.
8. *Acknowledge accomplishments.* When someone does something well, extend recognition.
9. *Be tactful and constructive.* With failure or wrongdoing, correct tactfully and constructively. Making friends is productive, creating enemies is destructive.
10. *Don't be a dictator.* If you properly balance responsibility, authority and capability, let people do their job. Then failure is only because of a disparity or your intrusion.
11. *Be the bigger person.* Acknowledge your failures, errors, bad decisions, faults, problems, etc. Don't blame someone else if it is you.
12. *Help others build their strengths.* Their success will be your success.
13. *Help others to live up to their potential and not your expectations.*

THE BOTTOM LINE

Motivating others that are a part of or can impact your business or personal life can lead to more and better work productivity and a higher level of personal achievement and satisfaction. You will get more out of your leisure activities, your home life, personal well being and your relationships will all improve. Your life will be more fulfilling and rewarding. Others probably will learn something but they also will definitely benefit by your support and personal attention. Motivate others to live up to their potential, for you. This is truly a win-win situation.

A. Answer to previous chapter question.
"Don't make my mistake, kid.
Don't follow orders your whole life.
Think for yourself."
Antz

Q. What movie are the following lines from?
"You're the only chance we've got!
Can you fly this plane and land it?"
"Surely you can't be serious?"
"I am serious, and don't call me Shirley."

Skills You Must Master to Succeed

CHAPTER FOURTEEN

Being a Good Negotiator

"The fellow who says he'll meet you halfway usually
thinks he's standing on the dividing line."

— Orlando A. Battista

WEBSTER'S
"To settle or arrange by conferring or discussing."

MINE
"To reach an agreement that achieves your desired results while
leaving the other believing that they have achieved theirs."

The art of negotiation has been described as *"a dance where you try to avoid stepping on the other person's toes."*

Many people are afraid to negotiate. They think negotiating requires confrontation, an adversarial relationship, being mean or demanding. All might possibly happen at some point but normally does not. Negotiation simply means arriving at the best possible deal that you can get and then deciding if you want it.

We all are exposed to negotiating beginning at a very young age when our parents offer us one thing in exchange for another. With this educational lesson, we start developing and honing our negotiating skills and the intrinsic style upon which they are founded.

The first form of negotiation is *assertive or aggressive negotiation*. This would include a passive-aggressive confrontation, a take it or leave it position, and intends to dominate the other side with intimidation making them uncomfortable, uncertain and insecure. This style of negotiating can develop when one side has a superior or advantageous position over the other and is devoid of any interest in the other person. Aggressive negotiation will usually result in a relationship that can not be repaired and, therefore, there is no expectation of a continuing relationship to ever exist. For example, this would be employed during a plea bargain discussion with a criminal defendant.

The second form of negotiation is *cooperative negotiation*. This involves developing mutual goals, understanding and more openness while still pursuing your individual best possible position. Opposite from the aggressive negotiation, you will put yourself in the other persons position and try to understand their issues and concerns. This is prevalent in sales, contractual situations or personal relationships with expected continued repeat contact.

In any negotiation, one side is usually stronger than the other. The stronger negotiator will know where they are going and will lead and dictate the pace and direction for the other side to follow. The stronger side will develop and arise out of experience, knowledge of details, being informed and having credibility.

You must make sure you are the stronger negotiator.

Negotiation doesn't necessarily require compromise or finding the win-win solution. It is finding a way to achieve the best possible deal for your side. There is no failure in negotiating. *"No"* is an acceptable outcome.

Consider the following negotiation guidelines:

Know your range of acceptable outcomes. Decide in advance your range of acceptable outcomes. Identify what really matters to you and your best case scenario. Identify where you can compromise if necessary and where you cannot. Also, know what your worst case acceptable scenario is and don't accept any less or you will be negative about the outcome, yourself and your handling of the negotiation and possibly not follow through with commitments made.

Have something of value. You must have something of value to offer or give to the other side that they want, or at least they believe there is value.

Really listen. Most people get distracted during negotiation from really listening to the other person because they are simultaneously having an inner dialogue in their mind. You cannot effectively listen internally and externally at the same time and be a superior negotiator. If you are talking internally, you will miss key issues or concerns of the other person that must be addressed. You will miss nonverbal communication like voice inflections, facial expressions and other body language communications that are important.

Ask questions. Questions help disclose and understand the needs, concerns and interest of the other party.

Be considerate. Being demanding of or condescending to the other person will not get you far in negotiation. Barking orders and ultimatums have abruptly ended many negotiations. Everyone deserves to be treated with respect and you will be rewarded in the end.

Think. The better you anticipate the position of the other party, the more prepared you are. The better you anticipate what the other party thinks you want, the better prepared you are.

Know your strengths. Even if the other party has a position of power, they are not all powerful and don't give away your strengths. You have something they want or they would not be there. You will always have the internal power of self confidence, experience and resourcefulness, even if external power dynamics are beyond your control, like changing technology, etc. change.

Maintain control. If the other person becomes irrational, angry or hostile, don't play their game. Stay calm, firm and controlled. They will settle down after their temper tantrum fails to elicit a response. Such actions are probably intentional anyway. Even if they move to leave, let them. After they calm down, they will return or contact you to continue and after their behavior has failed, it will most likely not happen again.

BATNA. Research on negotiation from the Harvard Negotiation Project developed this acronym that stands for *Best Alternative To A Negotiated Agreement.* Know what your options are, the alternatives and pros and cons of the choices. Can you walk away? Also consider the BATNA of the other party.

There is no failure. If the negotiation does not have an acceptable mutually agreeable conclusion, just say "No." This is not a failure and a polite and amicable separation is often an invitation to another possible future attempt. In addition, this is often an expected and necessary part of the negotiation process.

In addition, in a sales negotiation when you are the prospective purchaser:

Understand the salesperson. The salesperson's primary job is to make the sale. Secondly, they want to get the highest possible price for their product. Ultimately though, they would rather make the sale at the lowest possible price rather than lose the sale altogether.

Make sure they know you are serious. If the salesperson does not know you are serious, they will not put their full effort into the sale. Show them how serious you are by asking specific questions instead of general questions.

Don't be anxious. Being anxious tells the salesperson you will probably buy no matter what and, therefore, you will probably not get the best price or deal. Salespeople are trained to sell. Make them do their job.

Don't show your hand. If you tell them what you want up front, you might actually get it when you could have done better. Making an offer without fully knowing or understanding their position could be assuming concessions that you may not need to make.

Patience. Be patient. Often salespeople keep their best offers until the end, only to be used if needed.

Be able to walk away. If the price or terms are not right and you are not able to walk away, you will not be an effective negotiator.

Negotiation is utilized at work with employment; coworkers, developing contracts or agreements, sales and purchasing. You use negotiation to settle issues with family, friends and neighbors. You negotiate purchases or sales of homes, cars and other items. You negotiate terms of personal relationships for social and entertainment interaction. You use negotiation with teachers, employers, almost everyone.

What is at least one reason why some people are paid large amounts of compensation and receive other benefits while others do not? They retain people who are professional negotiators. For example, CEO's, business executives, athletes, celebrities, all have professional negotiators (agents) or they themselves have learned to be strong negotiators.

Negotiation is a fluid process not a moment. Being a good negotiator is a result of experience, practice and a learned application of strategies and skills. With each negotiation, you will learn something that will make you more successful with the next negotiation. These progressive successes will improve your skills in facilitating desired results. The best negotiator is one that is actually enjoying themselves with the process.

A GOOD NEGOTIATOR

1. *Develop your range of outcomes* from best case to worst case. Don't settle for any less than worst case.
2. *Have something of value* that the other side wants.
3. *Really listen* to the other side, what they say and their body language.
4. *Ask questions* to understand their needs and concerns so they are addressed.
5. *Be considerate.* Being demanding or condescending will not encourage the most from the other party.
6. *Think* about the other person's position and what they may think yours is.
7. *Know your strengths* and don't give them up.
8. *Maintain control* even when the other party might not.
9. *BATNA.* Know your **B**est **A**lternative **T**o **A** **N**egotiated **A**greement.
10. *There is no failure.* "No" is an acceptable conclusion.
11. *The stronger negotiator will lead* in the direction they want while the weaker follows. Be the stronger negotiator.

SALES NEGOTIATION

1. *Understand the salesperson.* Ultimately, his goal is to make the sale even at a lesser profit.
2. *Let them know you are serious* in order to get their total and best effort.
3. *Don't be anxious.* They will know and you will probably not get the best deal.
4. *Don't show your hand.* Tell them what you want and you may get it, making concessions needlessly.
5. *Be patient.* Negotiation is a process, not a moment.
6. *Be able to walk away.* If you are able to walk away when the best deal possible is not what you wanted, you will be the most effective negotiator.

THE BOTTOM LINE

Success will follow the stronger negotiator. The stronger negotiator will lead, dominate and control the direction a negotiation takes and requires experience which takes practice. Negotiation requires preparation and knowledge of all issues on both sides of the deal. Most negotiation is cooperative negotiation. You must listen and ask questions to fully understand and appreciate the other sides concerns so that they may be addressed to accomplish your desired results. There is no failure in walking away and saying *"No"*.

A. Answer to previous chapter question.

"You're the only chance we've got.

Can you fly this plane and land it?"

"Surely you can't be serious?"

"I am serious, and don't call me Shirley."

Airplane

CHAPTER FIFTEEN

Managing Roadblocks

"Once I decide to do something, I can't have people telling me I can't. If there's a roadblock, you jump over it, walk around it, crawl under it."

— Kitty Kelly

W E B S T E R ' S

"A situation or condition preventing further progress toward a goal."

M I N E

"A temporary and manageable challenge possibly delaying but not preventing progress."

I am sure you have heard the old joke: A couple driving to Disney World sees a sign that reads, **"DISNEY WORLD LEFT"** so they turned around and went home.

This may be an example of a roadblock that did not exist and was created simply from misunderstanding or misinterpretation. The traveling couple created the roadblock that prevented them from reaching their goal, to visit Disney World.

There are many times when pursuing a project or goal that, at any given moment, a perceived major roadblock is encountered. However, after time and thought, this roadblock is dwarfed to a mere and manageable interference, interruption or small delay.

A consumer products distribution Company with rented warehouse facilities at maximum capacity, negotiates a major contract with a new product manufacturer. After several failed attempts to locate additional available warehouse space, they were about to cancel the contract. The company discovers it can purchase a larger facility to accommodate their needs and the total ownership costs will be less than what the total rental costs for existing and additional warehouse would have been.

How you recognize and manage roadblocks will determine your Personal Success.

Roadblocks should be accurately recognized, identified and defined. You will then be able to classify roadblocks that you will: Avoid, Remove, Go Over, Under, Around, or Through.

Consider an airplane. Once you have a reported storm in the path of your flight, you will:

First – Confirm that there is actually a storm. Then, once confirmed, your choices are:

A. Change your course to AVOID the storm.
B. Increase your altitude to GO OVER the storm.
C. Decrease your altitude to GO UNDER the storm.
D. Change your course to go AROUND the storm.
E. Stay on course and go THROUGH the storm.

The action you take will be based upon information gathered, such as the storms strength, altitude, size, safety, delay time, etc. The storm would certainly be an obstacle, however, it would not prevent your arrival at your destination, just possibly delay it. Unfortunately, in this analogy to REMOVE the storm is not possible.

The first step is to make sure that the actual roadblock is properly identified before investing time and effort to remove it.

Mark and Karen were told by their new home builder that the closing on their home would be delayed for several days awaiting the County issuance of the Certificate of Occupancy (CO). They had all of their possessions packed in a moving van, so they kept asking questions. Since Mark knew some County people, he continued to push for a name of the person to contact to try and work out the delay. Finally, the builder admitted that the only reason the CO was not being issued was because the builder had not yet paid the impact fees required prior to the County issuing the CO. Now embarrassed, the builder hand delivered a check to the County within two hours and the closing occurred on time. This made Mark very happy, not only to close and move into their new home but, and more importantly, avoiding the wrath of Karen.

Roadblocks, although occurring naturally, are often created by yourself or others by laziness, blaming or faulting others, avoidance of work, lack of motivation, and excuses for failures or even may be intentionally created by others that want to see you fail.

Whatever the source, the important thing to remember is to properly identify the true roadblock before implementing your planned action to succeed.

For many examples, all you need to do is watch the news for those real life human interest stories:

Double amputee pursues and masters rock climbing hobby.

Blind mountain climber reaches summit of Mount Everest.

Skinny tattooed long greasy haired band member marries beautiful model.

Techno-Geek transcends social status and gets prom date with beautiful popular girl. (This did happen!)

When reading about the life of Thomas Edison, it seems that he was told a couple thousand times that he could not make a light bulb, until he did.

MANAGING ROADBLOCKS

1. *Make sure* that a roadblock actually exists.
2. *Identify and determine* what the roadblock really is.
3. *Once identified,* determine how to handle it:
   A. *Avoid it.* Find another course of action.
   B. *Remove it.*
   C. *Go around it.*
   D. *Go over it.*
   E. *Go under it.*
   F. *Go through it.*

Be the airplane!

THE BOTTOM LINE

Roadblocks are a fact of life. There are almost always roadblocks attempting to keep you from reaching your goals. You must progress through, over, under, around, remove or avoid them. How well you manage this will determine how quickly and efficiently you achieve your own Personal Success.

Q. What movie is the following line from?

"Forget it Murphy.

Roadblocks can't stop something

that can't be stopped."

CHAPTER SIXTEEN

Being An Innovator

"Learning and innovation go hand in hand. The arrogance of success is thinking that what you did yesterday will be sufficient for tomorrow."

— William Pollard

WEBSTER'S

"To start or introduce something new."

MINE

"To see or find a new, creative or different and better way that others can't, don't or won't and boldly apply it with success."

The successful person is one that thinks *"outside the box"*. They take their training, education and experiences when looking at something and think *"How can this be done better?"*

To be an innovator, you must make sure you understand what that means.

Improvement is when you take what you currently have and continue to do the same thing but make it or do it different and better.

To be an innovator is to discover new ways, methods or applications and make the necessary changes.

One story that I heard a long time ago that has always stuck with me, I think would be an example.

In the early days after the recipe for Coca-Cola was discovered and it was being dispensed in eateries and sandwich shops, the company was working to increase distribution and consumption. A man walked into the company offices and asked to meet with the President, which he did. The stranger told the President that for $10,000 he would tell him how Coca-Cola's profits could be increased dramatically. The President responded that he would pay the money after hearing the idea and if he believed it would increase sales. The gentleman nodded in agreement and said only two words, "Bottle it." The President of Coca-Cola wrote the gentleman a check for $10,000.

To be an innovator you must be creative. *Creativity is the mother of invention* (innovation). However, you can be creative without being an innovator. A sculptor can create a beautiful piece of art with the same work tools and techniques that have been used by others. His art work would be creative but not innovative.

Unfortunately, our innovative creativity has been suppressed because of education and training in a controlled environment. We are taught rules, given procedures and restrictions, trained to do things a certain and specific way. Have you ever heard, *"This is the way we have been shown (or taught) to do it"* or *"Because we have always done it this way."* To be creative, you must overcome this.

Our environment affects our innovative abilities. Naturally, if we lived in an environment that was conducive to and encouraged innovation it would come more easily. Most likely, your environment, particularly at work, is not conducive to creativity and innovation.

However, you can affect your work environment and certainly have a creative environment outside of work and can be open to creative and innovative thoughts and ideas regardless of your surroundings.

Your limitations will be different from someone else's. Your boundaries will be when you start seeing restrictions and barriers or impossibilities. *"There is no way this can be completed on time."* Whereas, being an innovator would be *"What must be done differently in order to meet the deadline?"*

The concept of brainstorming would be employed. Think of and consider any and all possibilities no matter how impossible, ridiculous or far fetched they may seem. What was inconceivable before may be very possible now, especially considering technological advancements or simply applying a different perspective.

Try living in a creative and innovative environment.

> *Practice being creative.* Begin by looking at small every day problems you deal with. How can they be dealt with that would be more efficient, economical, practical or even eliminated. What isn't happening that could be better or what is that is counterproductive. What changes could be made. Analyze the need.
>
> *Identify and remove creative constraints where possible.* Work constraints can be addressed to whatever degree is within your authority. Home and personal constraints you can control. Most importantly, remove constraints within your own thinking.
>
> *Utilize brainstorming.* Be open to and seriously consider any and all ideas from any source no matter how impossible or

ridiculous they may seem. Velcro was originally disregarded as a useless product development by manufacturers. The discovery of oil by farmers in the USA was originally considered problematic to ranchers and farmers. A small town in Canada once viewed the annual migration of Polar Bears through their town as an irritation until they realized that by publicizing this fact resulted in profit from tourist dollars that established the towns primary source of income.

Be receptive to ideas. Often innovative ideas will be presented from an unexpected source. I understand that Cell phones were made smaller when Prince Charles made the comment at a presentation *"...can't you fold them in the middle or something?"* Be prepared with paper and pencil or personal recorder to note ideas when they occur. Often a brilliant thought not written down at the moment of inception will fade and be lost to time and subsequent distractions.

Avoid restrictions. Avoid people, groups, teams or jobs that are not receptive to creativity and innovation. Someone that always responds *"That's a dumb idea."* is going to be a put down and a constant negative influence. A workplace environment that does not reward or appreciate creative input will have limited, if any, growth and advancement potential.

Challenge your mind. Read, scan and research publications, literature, existing ideas from the internet and trade journals and from the library. Be a catalyst for creative discussions with your peers and coworkers.

Change your lifestyle. Sitting at your computer, desk or in front of the television can create mental stagnation. Exercise increases oxygen and adrenaline in your system and this will be mentally stimulating. (This is not contrary to challenging your mind.) Listening to relaxing music can allow your mind to wander and be receptive to new ideas or approaches.

Successful people are creative and innovative people. They overcome limitations and constraints to find a better way. They look beyond the limitations that others see as impenetrable barriers.

We all have the potential to be an innovator once we realize the need and rewards.

As I once read somewhere, *"You learn to solve problems by solving problems."*

BE AN INNOVATOR

1. *Practice being creative.*
2. *Identify and remove creative constraints.*
3. *Utilize brainstorming.*
4. *Be receptive to new ideas.*
5. *Avoid restrictions.*
6. *Challenge your mind.*
7. *Change your lifestyle.*

THE BOTTOM LINE

To be an innovator requires a person to apply themselves and think beyond what they have been taught. To explore and exploit possible answers after others have accepted their limitations. An innovator is always challenging themselves after others have stopped. There are only two choices in life: stand still or move. As Albert Einstein put it, *"Imagination is more important than knowledge."*

A. Answer to previous chapter question.

"Forget it Murphy.
Roadblocks can't stop something
that can't be stopped."

The Wraith

Q. What movie is the following line from?

"If everybody is thinking alike
then somebody isn't thinking."

CHAPTER SEVENTEEN

Impressions

"Impressions are immediate; change is evolutionary."

— Mark C. Middleton

WEBSTER'S

"An effect, feeling, or image retained as a result of experience."

MINE

"That lasting individual memory, feeling, emotion or belief transmitted or communicated consciously or subconsciously by everything we are, say, do and how we react, behave and conduct ourselves in all aspects of our lives."

Not just first impressions, you make impressions through almost every aspect of your life whether you are aware of it or not. Successful people are sensitive to and aware of impressions that they make and, therefore, at least can somewhat direct them.

Those impressions that you are not aware of can help or hurt you even more than the ones you are aware of.

According to *California State University,* when you first meet people in an initial conversation they probably *"...decide if (s)he likes you in the first 5 seconds."*

From research for his book *Blink,* author Malcolm Gladwell determined that most people decide within the first fifteen seconds whether they like someone they meet for the first time or not.

So, somewhere between five and fifteen seconds must be correct.

The conclusion of multiple studies has determined that within four minutes of first meeting another individual and engaging them in conversation, you form judgments about that person based upon the following:

55%   Visual, i.e. Appearance, dress, posture, facial expressions.

38%   Tone of voice. Speech pattern, enunciation, accent, pace of speech and pleasantness of voice.

7%   Conversation quality. Quality of what you say, word skills, grammar.

According to a November 2003 survey by *Yahoo! Autos:* 52% of US people surveyed judge your level of success by the car you drive.

According to *Women's Entertainment Television,* in a recent poll of women, the number one ranking item that women look at for a first impression from a man is his shoes. I wouldn't have guessed that one and immediately went shopping.

As a personal experiment, I purchased a new pair of quality dress shoes. I wore them to a lunch date with my daughter. Sure enough, within a minute or two of meeting, she said, *"Nice shoes. Are they new?"*

The *Chicago Smell & Taste Treatment and Research Foundation* concluded that people with foul odors probably won't thrive in personal or career pursuits. The Olfactory Lobe, the area of the brain that processes smells, connects to the Limbic System which is in control of emotions. They established that *"...pleasant scents influence people to be in a happy state, and unpleasant odors tend to induce aggression."*

Coworkers and others responded favorably to people that smell pleasant and were pleasing. They wanted them to be successful. However, if you emit an offensive odor, the impression you will give others is that you are bad, even if it is subconsciously. According to the *Foundation* they found that people are likely to think something like, *"She does a great job, but I don't like her."*

I cannot quote the source but I heard about a recent study that determined individuals with pleasant and pleasing or comforting voices were provided more opportunity for sexual activity than those whose voices were not pleasant or pleasing.

Impressions are so important that it cannot be overstated. We all should be aware that every day we are making impressions with others that will project the kind of individual we are, the discipline and quality of our work, our morals and beliefs and how sincere we are about them.

I am sure we all recognize that we make impressions but I suspect that you are not aware to the extent you are scrutinized by others. In dealing with successful people, it has been a real education to learn how far they go to size up a person before they do business with them or their company, become associates or even socialize with someone.

There are professionals that consult on the right clothes to wear, hairstyle, etc. to project the impression desired. These professionals are retained by attorneys for their clients before entering a courtroom. Take a look at the before and after pictures of most any defendant in criminal court. Consultants are retained by politicians, celebrities and high profile business leaders. They recognize the importance of projecting the right impression. They also realize that the impression they are making in many cases will be analyzed by the press and public.

A Company whose employees deal with the public every single day **requires** *their high profile, high visibility employees have their hair trimmed every five days.*

I had an astute wealthy female client that met with an investment stock broker adviser for the first time and then I met with her afterwards. I asked her about the meeting and she replied, *"The seat of his pants were shiny and the diamond on his finger is fake. A woman notices these things."* She did not retain his services.

In interviews with the executive staffs of large Corporations, they all agree that poor grammar can create a barrier to advancement. As one President put it, *"It simply reflects a low level of professionalism."*

The advice of Laurie Schloff, *Director of Executive Coaching at Speech Improvement Co.,* a speech coach, in addition to using proper grammar:

1. Do not use vulgarity.
2. Avoid slang.
3. Employ more formal language during meeting.

Other advice of speech coach's is:

> Do not use wimpy language, like *"I think."*
> Do not say *"You know"* or *"Uh"* when speaking.
> Be confident not tentative when speaking.
> Avoid teen-speak, *"like, so cool."*
> Speak clearly and be articulate.

Your handwriting can reveal a great deal. Some companies now have an administrative position: Chief Graphology Officer. This person is an expert in the study of and interpretation of handwriting. This person assists in making a final decision on new employment applicants, based upon their handwriting. They can determine sincerity, intelligence and integrity, as well as other characteristics.

I knew a Company recruiter that, after an interview, would watch a prospective employee walk out to the parking lot to see the vehicle the interviewee was driving. I asked him *"Why?"* He responded, *"I don't care what he drives but I want to see how he takes care of it."* His philosophy was that a person that was sloppy and negligent about the appearance of their car probably was sloppy and negligent about their personal appearance and work ethics and product.

Most professionals commonly review their clients as to their personal and business operations in order to assure their own reputation. If that client doesn't measure up to the standards of their professional requirements, they terminate the relationship. Otherwise, in the event a bad client is identified by legal, regulatory or negative public exposure, their other clients are put under a microscope of scrutiny.

There are just so many things in so many ways that you may or may not be aware of that provide an impression of who and what you are. You need to always be sensitive to the impression you are giving.

In part, you as a person and your character and morals will be judged by:

Your speech, grammar, appearance and hygiene.
The character and behavior of your spouse.
The behavior and manners of your children.
The condition of your home, inside and out.
The condition of your automobile.
The condition, fashion and appropriateness of your clothing.

Your personal conduct, morals and behavior.
Your family, friends and associates.
Your profession, business relations and conduct.
Personal hobbies and interests.
How you care for your pets.

The following are some real case examples.

Intelligent and skillful attorney with failing legal practice and does not reach his business potential.

Jimmy has a professional office located in an old remodeled residence. The exterior needs painting and roof work. The parking area consists of cracked and broken, pothole asphalt. The landscaping is virtually nonexistent with extensive weeds for a lawn. The outside front door exterior surface is cracked and flaking and an old rusting paint can sits on the side of the entry where it has been in the same position for months.

Inside, the office waiting area is frayed carpet with the seams separating and in desperate need of replacement. The waiting area is furnished with extremely worn furniture that has some holes, and the wall paneling is partially separating from the walls. The receptionist desk and counters have several stacks of files with papers sliding out falling onto the surface. Behind the desk are several items of old and outdated and unused equipment sitting on the floor against the wall. All of the interior offices are permeated with the smell of stale tobacco smoke.

What would be your impression of this professional?

Small business success.

A small business that succeeds and thrives against several larger, more established competitors. The building and property is always maintained and clean. The inside is attractively decorated including some functional antiques. The interior is warm, inviting and comfortable. The employees are always smiling and cheerful. They always have quality (not generic) refreshments available.

The owners are particular about personal and vehicle appearance, business presentation and they employ like individuals. The company provides training to employees on how they are expected to deal with business and customer relationships in person and over the telephone. They require that the work be done completely, correctly and timely.

The owners seek out people and businesses with similar ethics and discipline.

Successful individual.

Where we previously lived, my neighbor James was diligent about his home appearance and the maintenance of the house, yard and vehicles. We engaged James's company for some work. His work was impeccable showing the same diligent attention to completeness and detail. Not only will we use James again but we will naturally give him a glowing referral to others.

Family impression loses business

Scotty is a personable real estate agent that lives in a large community where there are commonly several homes listed for sale. Scotty does not get a single listing when other real estate agents repeatedly do. Unfortunately for him, his ten year old son often plays in the driveway in front of their home with a CD player set up in the open garage loudly playing rap music that contains vulgar, violent and offensive lyrics. Scotty apparently does not appreciate the impression that his son makes by, first – owning such a CD (at his age or any age), second – playing it loudly in public, third – parents that would permit him to have such a CD, forth – the child as a reflection of the parents. Scotty's son has alienated the residents with the impression he gives costing Scotty listings.

Put this to the test, I did. I dealt briefly with an individual that did very sloppy work. He was loud and abrasive with others, quick to blame his shortcomings and failures on someone else's actions and became hostile or even angry easily. He was constantly late for appointments and had a *"My way or the highway"* attitude.

I drove by his home. His yard was a disaster. It was not maintained to the point of extensive dirt and weeds. Junk was located in front of and behind the home. The garage door was open revealing an equally disastrous condition inside. Tools and equipment scattered around with stacks of materials and boxes that had fallen over. Several bags of garbage were stacked along the wall, and all were covered with dirt. I stopped and spoke briefly with one of his two sons. The boy (probably about age twelve) was rude and openly vulgar.

Since I find dealing with or even tolerating the presence of this type of counterproductive person, I choose not to include them as associates or friends and excluded this person from my list.

We all make our own choice of the kind of people we surround ourselves with in business and socially.

The philosophy of a successful President and CEO of the company that she started, created and built. During a conversation, she disclosed that one of her favorite ways to size up the character of a person is to play golf with them. As she states, while they spend about four hours together, she looks to see if they cheat, gloat when winning, swear after a bad shot, get angry, throw their golf clubs, blame the course or others for a bad shot, are assistive/constructive, dwell on a prior poor shot to the detriment of the current shot, etc. As she said, "You can really size up their character." The sportsmanship character will reflect how that person will perform in business and as an individual.

"Those of greater character will face greater challenges."
—Mark C. Middleton

Individual impressions and facts provided by multiple sources build and support your overall conclusion about a person and you should not depend on any one source or impression.

"The eye sees not itself but by reflection..."
—Shakespeare

IMPRESSIONS

1. *Your physical appearance and fashion.*
2. *Your personal hygiene.*
3. *Your grammar and speech pattern.*
4. *Your personal conduct and morals.*
5. *Your personal lifestyle – shopping, eating, etc.*
6. *What you drive and its appearance.*
7. *Family, friends, business relations.*
8. *Where you were educated and to what level.*
9. *Your home furnishings and care, inside and out.*
10. *Your profession and business conduct.*
11. *Your hobbies, interest and vacation choices.*
12. *Your pets and how you care for them.*
13. *Your religion and level of commitment.*
14. *Every aspect of your life.*

THE BOTTOM LINE

We are all aware of and prepare for times when we make impressions. You are often not aware of those times and what things people will look at that will form an impression that they will use to make a judgment about you. Everything about you and your life personally, how you live it and your choices of relationships will divulge information about you. You will disclose your true self. You should know what that is. You must make a conscious decision to be aware of and sensitive to those impressions whether you acknowledge them or not. Others will and they are.

The best advice is to actually become the person that you hope other people will think you are. Then the impressions will be automatic, natural and favorable. Otherwise, people will see who you really are, and aren't.

A. Answer to previous chapter question.
"If everybody is thinking alike then somebody isn't thinking."
Patton

Q. What movie is the following line from?
"When you first entered the restaurant, I thought you were handsome ...
And then, of course, you spoke ..."

Implementation

CHAPTER   EIGHTEEN

Impulse Decisions

"Don't let other people tell you what you want."

— Pat Riley

WEBSTER'S

"Tending to act by spontaneous urge or inclination rather than by thought."

MINE

*"An action taken based upon the moment without benefit
of thoughtful consideration that later reviewed could or should
have been done better, different or not at all."*

Successful people avoid making impulse decisions. They invest time and resources before making a well considered and informed decision.

Marketing products or services is highly effective when an environment or feeling of immediacy or urgency to act or purchase is created. Impulse purchases are triggered by the candy, gum and magazines with sensational headlines or pictures of beautiful people at the checkout counter or the products placed at eye level and with eye catching color, characters or designs in the stores. The telemarketers with the limited time or product offer requiring an immediate commitment and decision over the telephone. The automobile salesperson that holds the keys to your trade-in car and a *"good-faith check"* and presses for a decision prior to your leaving the dealership to prevent comparison shopping or taking a day to make a considered decision. The salesperson striving for a deposit check or signature before you leave is pressuring you to make an impulse decision.

J. Jeffrey Inman of the University of Wisconsin and Russell S. Winer of the University of California at Berkeley did research which combined data from a Point of Purchase Institute study and recorded the following results, in summary:

Analyzing over 30,000 purchases, by 4,200 consumers in 14 cities, the average shopping trip results in 54% unplanned purchases and big shopping trips resulted in 68% unplanned purchases. In a store that you go down all of the aisles, over 67% of your purchases are by impulse compared to about 50% impulse purchases when visiting only some of the aisles. In-aisle displays attract 58% impulse purchases, where end of aisle displays attract 61% impulse purchases and checkout counter displays attract 64% impulse purchases.

They all know that, given time to consider all the pros and cons, you quite likely will not purchase. The salesperson keeps you focused on the benefits of the positive points to keep you from considering the negatives. The automobile salesperson, during discussion, refers to the prospective purchase as "your car". *"We can have your car ready for you to drive home in 30 minutes."*

How many people wait to be told what they like, want or need?

Do you wait for the reviews on a movie to be told whether it is any good?

Do you listen to the movie advertisements quoting somebody (?) that this is the *"Best picture of the year."*

Must you be told by an ad that you must have or need a product or service?

Studies have been done and continue to be done to determine what triggers a person to make a purchase. The more successful Companies have it down to an art form. They attack all five senses. They make it look desirable, smell wonderful, feel sensual, sound pleasurable and, when appropriate, taste delightful. They tell you that you want or need *"IT"*.

According to Paco Underhill in his book *"Call of The Mall"* two-thirds of what you purchase in a store you had no intention to buy prior to entering.

According to recent studies, 35% of Burger King sales were a result of road signs triggering an impulse decision. On-premise point-of-purchase store signs resulted in an average increase in the number of sales, the average dollar value per sale and the average number of items per sale. Pole signs increased total sales by an average of 8.6%.

It is not a coincidence while walking through a mall you are immersed in the aroma of cookies, pretzels and other foods. How many barbecue houses have you been anywhere nearby when there isn't the smell of barbecued something cooking over a fire with the smoke and aroma bellowing from a chimney?

When selling a new home, not only is the model furnished by professionals attuned to popular styles, fabrics and colors, it will also have the smell of fresh cookies in the kitchen or popcorn in the game room. The sales office will have comfortable seating with an assortment of refreshments and pleasant music. With consideration, they will fight for that deposit check, especially for a specific lot thereby preventing someone else from the purchase while you decide, thus creating a sense of urgency.

Anyone who has purchased a new vehicle with a trade-in vehicle has gone through this experience. The salesperson takes your keys so they can properly assess the value of your car to give you the optimum trade-in amount (yeah right). You notice that you don't get your keys back before spending arduous time consuming negotiation of the price. They also request a *"good-faith"* check of say one hundred dollars when they present your offer to their manager to 'fight' for you and show that you are serious (they assume the average consumer is a total idiot). That keeps you from easily leaving, which they are critical to prevent. That would provide you time to comparison shop or to consider all the reasons against your purchase.

Telemarketers of products, services or contributions also work by impulse decisions. They work for a commitment before you hang up the telephone. My suggestion is to NEVER commit to anything by telephone. Require them to mail you any information they like but do not commit to the purchase of products, services or contributions over the telephone.

Also, NEVER provide personal information over the telephone. If they are legitimate, they can read the information (Name, address, telephone number, etc.) to you and you can confirm whether it is correct or not, if you choose to do so. Never provide name, address or other information to someone you do not know and NEVER provide social security or drivers license numbers information by telephone.

Impulse decisions are not limited to purchases.

Many of us make an impulse decision related to employment, marriage, divorce, where to live, disciplining a child or animal. Don't let your emotions take over or be maneuvered into a position of having to make a quick, impulse decision. Wait until you are not angry, caught up in the moment or maybe intoxicated. Take time to intelligently look at all the angles. This is not to say that you will make a different decision, just a more thoughtful complete and correct one.

So many times I deal with people that, in hindsight, they had all the information needed but made the wrong decision after reacting by impulse or emotion. They were driven by greed, sex, desire, materiality, whatever. Too many times people look back and say, *"I sure didn't think that completely through."* Or *"I wish I could go back and change that."*

Have you ever disciplined a child while angry and later realized that you were physically too severe? Have you ever struck an animal when angry and caused serious harm or injury, physical or mental? Have you ever struck another person when angry?

Why did this happen? Because of impulse decisions. You made an emotional impulse decision and instantly reacted instead of waiting until you were thinking rationally, looking at the situation and causes, and then deciding an appropriate response.

Business managers that have achieved the highest degree of Personal Success are those that can think quickly but take the time necessary to internally and externally process all available information and consider all the alternatives before making a fully informed final decision, thus avoiding reacting impulsively.

Occasionally, an opportunity may be lost due to delay. *"If you snooze, you lose."* However, the few missed beneficial opportunities will be far surpassed and financially rewarded by the avoided mistakes and losses.

During my practice, my better clients fortunately called me before making some commitments and I am happy to say that together we looked at all the information and can honestly say in hindsight, made the right decisions.

The following are some of the impulse decisions that were avoided.

Joe, a business client, was contacted by an individual wanting him to invest $5,000 for the purchase of some organic material that would be grown and the resulting product would be sold to a cosmetics company. The time to invest was limited and he was pressured to respond with a decision quickly. Joe contacted me and after discussions with him and the individual that approached him, I advised him not to invest, which he didn't. The company went bankrupt within a few months and all those that had invested, lost their money and were left with a product of no value that no one wanted.

William was contacted by an individual representing himself as a foreign government official looking to funnel excess oil excise tax revenue funds through an American checking account. William was to open an account with $25,000 and receive a 2% fee from oil funds deposited for providing this service. The foreign individual represented that there were millions of dollars involved. The signers of the account were to be William and this foreign individual. William was excited and ready to go to the bank and open the account the same day, but fortunately decided to talk to me first. I advised him to not participate, and, after much discussion, he did not. This was exposed as a scheme on a national scale shortly thereafter and had cost people many thousands of dollars. An impulse decision and action was pressured by greed.

A client, business owner was approached by an individual offering to purchase his entire company for $500,000, which was a favorable price to my client. Bonds were to be used for the purchase and subsequently sold by my client. The client was ready to sell, had a contract prepared and then contacted me. Upon inspection, the bonds with face value of $500,000 due and payable several years in the *future, without interest, and upon making a call to a brokerage firm, it was determined that they had a current redemption or sales value of about $40,000.*

In each of the above actual cases it was represented that the offers or opportunities had a limited time, significant money to be made and it was critical for them to decide and act immediately. If the individuals had made an impulse decision they would have lost substantial amounts of money.

The following is a case where an impulse decision was made, and money lost.

An Investment advisor conducted a seminar that invited retiree's to attend. A corporation was to issue a limited amount of bonds at an annual interest rate of 14% at a time when the going rate was a range of 6-7%. There was no discussion about ratings as this was a small statewide company. Unfortunately, two of my clients invested at the seminar without consulting me. The company made the interest only payments in the beginning but within two years the company was bankrupt and the investment were worthless.

I would also like to offer another saying that has personally benefited myself and others and that I feel we should all keep in mind when considering any purchase.

———●◦●———

"Don't buy what you don't want."

—Unknown

———●◦●———

Much of the discussion has related to purchases or investments. The concept of Impulse decisions on relationships is also applicable. When possible, if you are being pressured to make a decision or take an immediate action, consider all the long term consequences or results. Before making a decision or taking any action, you should *PLAY IT SAFE:*

Proud of your decision..
Looks like the right decision.
Anxious to tell everyone else about it.
You feel good about your decision.

Intelligent decision.
Thought through as much as possible.

Sounds like the right decision.
Are happy with your decision.
Feels like the right decision.
Excited about your decision.

If it doesn't look right, feel right, sound right, taste right and smell right, then your decision cannot pass *The Smell Test*, and it probably *Stinks*.

The following real life examples are what may happen when someone makes an impulse decision that results in tragic consequences.

Susan was a popular and lovely young girl in High School. She was liked by most which, unfortunately, made her a target for a thoughtless and jealous less popular girl, Helen. One day during lunch, Susan was carrying her tray and set it down onto the table. She pulled out the chair to sit down, however, Helen was at the table behind her and thought it would be funny to move the chair further back just before Susan was to sit. Susan fell onto the hard floor landing on her tailbone. Susan sustained internal skeletal damage that prevented her from ever being able to bear a child.

John, a teenager, was riding with four of his friends one night when, to impress them, he decided it would be funny to throw a concrete block from the car at a car coming from the other direction. The block hit the windshield of the other car sending the female driver to the hospital requiring ten hours of surgery followed by several additional reconstructive surgeries and years of therapy. Her life is changed forever. John was caught and is facing twenty five years in prison.

We should stop and remember to **PLAY IT SAFE** when making decisions, especially impulse decisions, and make sure whatever decision you make or action you take can pass the **SMELL TEST**.

IMPULSE DECISIONS

1. *Know what your shopping needs are* before you go.
2. *Take time for comparison shopping.* Search for and compare alternatives.
3. *Always avoid high-pressure sales tactics* that require an immediate response or decision.
4. *Always recognize that you are being bombarded with advertising and solicitation* based upon triggering an impulse decision.
5. *Don't commit to any purchase or solicitation over the telephone* or by door-to-door salesman.
6. *Think for yourself.*

THE BOTTOM LINE

You are pressured to make impulse decisions every day. Always take time to consider the ramifications of your choices before making a final decision. If after some time you regret the decision you made, you probably made an impulse decision. Recognizing circumstances that create an impulse decision situation probably also means already knowing your answer. Never feel pressured by limited time offers, or influenced by possible missed opportunities, unrealistic financial rewards or intimidation. That is usually a sure sign that the other person is trying to tell you what you want. PLAY IT SAFE and put your decision to The Smell Test to make sure that it doesn't Stink.

A. Answer to previous chapter question.
"When you first entered the restaurant,
I thought you were handsome ...
And then, of course, you spoke ..."
As Good As It Gets

Q. What movie is the following line from?
"You know, there's a lesson here,
which is: never try to make
life or death decisions
when you're feeling suicidal."

CHAPTER NINETEEN

Organization

"With organization you build your future.
Without it you relive your past."

— Mark C. Middleton

WEBSTER'S
"To arrange or assemble into an orderly, structured, functional whole."

MINE
"Systemic procedures and/or processes in the management of people,
information or materials for optimal efficiency and accessibility."

Organization is a critical cornerstone in constructing your Personal Success.

Constructive work time will be wasted and stress will be created if you are not organized. Your thinking, approach, work space, support staff, equipment, transportation, etc., all are critical elements related to a well organized individual, office, business, home, family and personal relationships, your space, everything.

The people you most interrelate with will have a direct effect upon you and, therefore, how well they are organized will also impact your efficiency and stress level. To help yourself, you must also help others realize their need for organization.

Consider some of the following symptoms of disorganization in yourself or others:

Failure to get things done. Consistently not being able to complete your scheduled tasks or "to do" lists. Settling for a lesser degree of achievement or giving up altogether.

Failure in achieving goals. Not meeting goals because of running out of time, resources or missing needed opportunities to achieve those goals.

Time lost searching for things. Time spent searching for documents, letters, lists, notes, tools or whatever you need to do your work is time not spent being productive.

Not getting to appointments or places on time. Consistently being late for scheduled appointments or not being ready at the time you had committed to.

Re-creating what once was already created. Having to do work or research over because you cannot find what you had already done. Worse yet is to continue forward without it.

Disorganization creates stress.

I am emphasizing stress in relation to organization because about 300 billion dollars each year is spent and/or lost on stress related health care costs and work loss.

Consider the following steps to assist you in becoming more organized at home and/or work:

Develop a system. Being organized requires having a structured system in place that allows you to be able to find what you need when you need it and accomplish your actions and activities timely and without creating stress, frustration, crisis or chaos.

Centralize information and communication. You should have a central point for information receiving and communicating with others. This would be where important papers or bills would be organized and processed. You should also have calendars and appointment books for family members or work associates and bulletin boards, message pads for yourself and others around you. Having a message pad or *"while you were out"* note pads with a pen by the telephone.

Have a filing system. A filing system for home and office will keep all important documents, contracts, papers and letters filed by subject, individual or company for future reference and historical paper trail.

Have a storage and support system. Just as with a filing system, a storage system creates *"A place for everything and everything in its place."* In addition, a support system would be a tangible and intangible system to support your organizational *"tools"*. For example, you would not have a computer without a printer, a desk without a chair or files without a cabinet. Make sure you have what you need to make everything interface and work.

If your thinking and approach are disorganized, you will spend unnecessary time for preparation and implementation which will translate to lost time, money, business and opportunity. For example,

The owner/manager of a company schedules a meeting with all of the staff to address business promotion and development. During the meeting, various staff raises questions pertaining to some business and some non-business issues unrelated to the meeting subject. The owner sidetracks from the meeting agenda and focus and engages in discussions about unrelated subjects. A meeting that should have been about an hour instead lasted three hours and concluded without formulating an action plan. The subject was left for a future meeting. Productive staff work time was lost and wasted and they failed develop and implement an effective plan thus delaying business promotion and development.

Organization and efficiency is achieved when people work at their highest level of expertise, capability and experience.

Organization can be compromised by lack of support staff. Imagine the loss of productivity that would result if a Doctor had to spend time to present and explain the various forms that have to be prepared by a new patient prior to examination, for the lack of a receptionist? The lack of a secretary to do the copying, filing and typing required for an attorney or accountant? You wouldn't want a salesman spending time in non-sales area of order processing.

All jobs are important, however, your time and energy should be focused on your highest level of capability and productivity. Others should also spend their time at the highest level of their capability either in supporting you or being supported by you.

Having the proper tools, equipment or vehicle for the job is, obviously, essential. In this business environment you would not even conceive of any professional without computers, cell phones, copy and fax machines, automobile, etc. Whatever your task, you should analyze it and determine what tools and equipment are necessary.

Take notice the next time you are at a business office. Signs of an organized (and presumably efficient) work area would be:

Equipment commensurate with work load. There should be sufficient filing cabinets for files and paperwork also cabinets and storage for office supplies and the proper equipment available for the defined tasks.

Individual work space. All individuals have their own work space, desk, room or office.

Contemporary equipment. Current equipment: computers, printers, fax machine, tools, supplies, books etc. Old and severely outdated equipment is not a good sign.

Timely response. When you ask a question about your particular situation, they are able to quickly retrieve your records and respond timely, accurately and completely to your inquiry or telephone call.

When you are dealing with a business, some signs that they may not be working efficiently thus costing them and you money, time, lost productivity, product or services and/or business may be:

Office clutter. Stacks of papers or files on desks, cabinets, tables or floor, especially if they are covered with a layer of dust. Office supplies stacked on tables, desks or floor. Unused equipment or supplies stored on floor under desks, tables or counters. Areas not maintained, unclean or disorderly.

Areas of disrepair. If the office is not maintained or has broken doors or cabinets, inoperative light fixtures or damaged ceilings or walls that have obviously been ignored for some time.

Insufficient work area for individuals. Individuals without their own work space maybe sharing desks or desk area.

Old equipment in use. Old outdated office equipment is simply inefficient compared to contemporary equipment, computers, copiers, printers, fax machines, etc.

Scattered papers falling out of files, folders or envelopes or stacked and not filed at all.

Untimely responses. When asking a question about your specific situation, they do not respond timely or respond without being familiar with your records or they do not return telephone calls timely.

Although the foregoing items deal with a business office, most would also apply to your own personal home and yours and your family's work areas within your home.

For yourself and your profession, you must analyze your transportation needs. If you are in sales, you want to have an appropriate vehicle that addresses your needs. For example,

A real estate salesperson shows up at an appointment to take a couple and tour several mid six figure homes for them to consider for purchase. He pulls up in an old, dirty compact car that has one of those token back seats suitable for seating one or two pygmies. (See chapter on impressions). Naturally, the couple ended up driving. The prospective buyers spent a token amount of time with the agent (only because they were too polite to blow him off immediately) then left and contacted another agent the next day. The salesman obviously failed to have the right tools for the job and lost a large commission ($30,000 plus) because of it, which probably has happened more than once to him.

You also need to be aware of some possible common myths of organization.

Being neat is being organized. Neatness is usually a sign of organization, however, it is easy to have neat piles or neat cabinets and still not be able to find things.

Cleanliness is organized. You can have the cleanest house in the community and still not be organized.

Having every minute scheduled is being organized. You do not have to schedule every minute. Time for spontaneity and the unexpected is necessary.

Being organized takes more time. Disorganization consumes time unnecessarily. Organization and scheduling assigns "just enough" time necessary to complete tasks, avoid unwanted obstacles and get things done. This will result in actually providing you more time in your day.

I am just not an organized person. Being organized is a decision and a choice. Once learned and applied, organization becomes habit: instinctive and automatic.

The organized person is one that wants to be ready and prepared to achieve **Personal Success.** Being organized is making a choice and once made, becomes more instinctive, automatic and natural. To the extent possible, you should also influence those you most interact with to also be organized. You will discover that you will have more time available, achieve your tasks and goals more easily and help relieve your life of a stress threat thus saving money, time and your health.

ORGANIZATION

1. *Develop a system* that enables you to find what you need when you need it.
2. *Centralize information and communication* for yourself and others you interact with.
3. *Have a filing system* for important documents, contracts, agreements, correspondence, etc.
4. *Have a storage system.* "A place for everything and every thing in its place."
5. *Help others* you commonly interact with become organized.

SIGNS OF DISORGANIZATION

1. *Failure to complete tasks* or "to do" lists.
2. *Failure to achieve goals.*
3. *Unable to locate things, papers, etc.*
4. *Failing to be on time* for appointments, meetings, personal commitments.
5. *Having to redo* what had already been done.

THE BOTTOM LINE

Organization is critical to competition, efficiency and productivity. The better organized you are the better you will be at each one individually and stronger as a whole. Your toughest competitor for your job, product, services or attention will be organized. Entering the battle without organization is preparation (oxymoron) for defeat. You will know it and others will quickly recognize and exploit your weakness. Organized people associate and move forward while disorganized people are left with each other searching for excuses.

A. Answer to previous chapter question.
"You know, there's a lesson here,
which is: never try to make
life or death decisions
when you're feeling suicidal."
Bulworth

CHAPTER TWENTY

Being Informed and Prepared

"Without proper preparation there can be no success"
— Robert Stevenson

WEBSTER'S
"Having information and being ready in advance for a particular purpose, event, or occasion."

MINE
"Assembling all possible and accessible pertinent information before making decisions, entering meetings, investing, acquiring or launching projects or taking actions."

To be informed is to be prepared
And
to be prepared is to be informed.

When making a decision about a purchase you do not want to rely on the opinion, recommendation, presentation or direction of the salesperson. Their motivation is almost always not your motivation.

When entering an office for a job interview, for example, wouldn't it be helpful to know about the Company products, annual sales, competitors, areas of distribution, Company history? Would it be helpful to know something about key Company personnel and maybe even the person interviewing you? Knowing their personal interests or hobbies, personal achievements, organization affiliations, family, etc.? This will provide you an insight for the interview, impress the interviewer and distinguish yourself from the multitude of others seeking the position.

Information is more readily available on almost everything and everybody than ever before in history. To be uninformed or unprepared is like saying to a salesman, *"I am totally lost and have no idea what I am doing. I am yours to take advantage of"* or saying to a job recruiter, *"This isn't really that important to me."*

How do you become informed and prepared? I am glad you asked because otherwise this would have been a very short chapter.

Here are some suggestions that may help you.

Discipline. Making and taking the time to do your homework. Research your subject or issue. Seek out others that may be more experienced or experts in the area you are dealing with. Be an information gatherer.

Have an open mind. When beginning research, don't seek out only information or data that supports a preconceived or desired result or answer. Be open to issues and avenues even though they may not be your own specific particular interest.

Be open minded and receptive to all material and then form your strategy or answer.

Keep your focus on the question. Understand and define what are the one or two most important issues. Do not get distracted by creating variables that monopolize time and effort. Don't get caught up in self created minutia. There are usually one or two issues that are the most important. Stay focused on them and everything else is reduced to simple details.

Make a large project a series of smaller projects. Some projects may appear overwhelming or you may be unable to decide where or how to begin. You can build on the completion of defined smaller projects in accomplishing the larger ones.

For example:

In looking at a prospective home purchase, you could help process the one big question "To purchase a specific home" with the completion of several smaller projects:

Contact the original builder and confirm the home specifications. If the home was built by a large builder, research the builder on the Internet.

Contact the County and verify property taxes, appraisal and valuation. Ask about future area development, new roads, communities, shopping centers, industrial parks.

Contact the local Sheriff's Department for crime statistics, area problems or other issues.

Contact the Homeowners Association and verify that there are no deed restriction violations, community sink hole history (Big issue in Florida), verify current assessment amounts, pending special assessments, etc.

Contact the existing insurance carrier and request a statement on the claim history.

Contact your insurance carrier and verify coverage availability with any possible exclusion. Insurance companies maintain extensive history on area sink holes, wind damage, flooding, etc.

You could research community home re-sales data for excessive turnover that may indicate a possible problem.

Drive through and/or park nearby the home on different days and at different times and observe community interactions.

Visit the neighborhood and meet some residents and talk to them about living in that community, local activities, area problems like flooding during rain, water quality, neighborhood problems, traffic issues and people issues.

Drive different routes on different days from your prospective home to work or shopping.

Contact lenders for pre-qualification, rates, options and terms.

Try finding a home that you are interested in and doing all of the above before contacting the real estate agent. While looking at the home, you will have fun with the agent and homeowner when they realize you know more about the home and location than they do.

Once you have assembled all the information obtained from your smaller defined projects, you will have what you need to make your larger, ultimate decision.

Get what you need. Especially in business, this concept is often violated. You may want to define your ultimate goal and work backwards to identify what is needed to achieve that goal. If you were opening a new business you would need to identify financial requirements, equipment, personnel needs, marketing, inventory and supplies, etc. Once you have your defined end goal, you can work backwards to see how you are going to satisfy those needs.

If you are unable to implement your plan or you know that what you need is not available, your plan has failed.

Listen. Learn from those that have mastered the art of listening. Professional interviewers like Dr. Phillip McGraw, Larry King, Barbara Walters, Oprah Winfrey; all are good listeners. Questions may be asked when the answer is not known or even when the answer is known. Each question builds and draws more information out. The Professional Interviewer can intentionally minimize their own knowledge to maximize the interviewees response thus extracting important information.

Don't word questions accusingly. *"What problems has the television been having?"* Is better than, *"What problems have you been having with the television?"* This would avoid the inference of possible personal fault.

In general, people are not used to actually being listened to. We all commonly greet someone with *"How are you doing?"* And the response is almost always *"I am doing fine."* The person asking usually doesn't care and the person responding knows it.

Often an initial response to a question only generates a positive answer. However, try following it up with a silent look and see if the other person then volunteers additional valuable and maybe problematic information that you would not have otherwise been able to get.

In consulting with a Company on implementing a financial reporting computer program, I asked the Controller, *"How is the system working?"* He quickly responded that everything was working fine. After a few seconds of silence as I continued to look directly at him, he then added, *"Well, we have been having a few problems with incomplete individual reports."* I asked about the problems and without further prompting from me, he provided valuable input to pass on to the Management Information Systems personnel for program changes. There are times when "Silence is golden."

Maintain a healthy skepticism. Do not accept things at face value. Often information details and facts are misrepresented. Sometimes this is from simple mistake, misunderstanding or miscommunication. However, often information, details or facts are presented and intentionally misrepresented, misquoted or misstated to create a desired "spin" on the issue or project. Develop a check-it-out-for-yourself discipline. This may merely verify what has been presented, however, often it will disclose a correction, difference or true piece of information or fact that will also be enlightening when sizing-up the person that misrepresented the information, fact, quote, detail, whatever. And, please believe me, this happens a lot!

When working with an out of state real estate agent, he provided pictures and a hand drawn map of a street with three homes for sale that, from the pictures and map, appeared to show expensive homes in an upscale area that backed up to a golf course. Upon visiting the area it was discovered that he had neglected to disclose on his map or verbally that between this upscale street and the golf course was an old low income residential area with a high crime rate and that in addition to the homes he had listed, there were also several other homes for sale on the same street. Apparently nobody wanted to live there.

Make your process a habit. Each time you find yourself informed and properly prepared for a situation, you add self-confidence. Self-confidence will always give you an advantage. When you are informed and prepared, others will accept your authority and you build more self-confidence. When you are not informed and prepared, your meaningful thoughts or ideas will be discounted resulting in possible loss of valuable input. You will be vulnerable like a prey in the presence of a predator.

Being informed and prepared with the best available information for whatever you will be facing is the very least you can do. If you aren't informed and prepared, how can success possibly follow? Success doesn't usually happen by chance, accident or to those that aren't able to recognize it.

"Every battle is won before it is ever fought."
—Sun-tzu, The Art of War

BEING INFORMED AND PREPARED

1. *Become disciplined* and take time to do your homework.

2. *Have an open mind* and don't begin with a predetermined answer seeking only for that which supports it.

3. *Keep focused on the question.* There are usually only one or two important issues. Don't get distracted by the small details.

4. *Accomplish large projects* by breaking them into a series of smaller one.

5. *Get what you need* for the defined desired outcome and work backwards to identify what must be known in order to accomplish it.

6. *Listen* to what others really say (or sometimes don't say) for valuable input.

7. *Maintain a healthy skepticism* and verify information (check-it-out-for-yourself). Don't accept things at face value or as presented to you.

8. *Make your process a habit.* You will build self-confidence with each success and self-confidence will then build more success.

THE BOTTOM LINE

Taking the time and making the effort to be as informed and prepared as you possibly can is the very least you can do. If you are not, everyone will know it and you lose credibility and seriousness. Practice at looking beneath the surface or reading between the lines. It often requires a special touch or approach to pierce the surface and extract pertinent valuable information.

Q. What movie is the following line from?
"My friend Harry and I are saving up money
for a pet store. I got worms!"

CHAPTER TWENTY-ONE

Well Planned Goals

"Obstacles are those frightful things you see when
you take your eyes off the goal."

— Hannay More

WEBSTER'S
"The objective toward which an effort or endeavor is directed."

MINE
"A defined conclusion for which the achievement is worth the cost to pursue."

Setting goals is a basic success tool used by athletes, business people, anyone that is driven to achievement. Goal setting establishes a focus for your long-term vision and helps sustain long-term and short-term motivation.

Your goals should be as well thought out, planned and defined and specific as possible. When appropriate, you should establish a series of small stepped goals that lead up to the achievement of a n ultimate goal. Goals should be realistically obtainable without being too easy or simple or so difficult that they become not realistically achievable.

Goals should be reviewed periodically, especially long-term goals. As you mature your priorities change, and your life experiences, circumstances and needs change and evolve. Goals may be redefined or even disappear with these changes, and you should let them, as they are redefined and replaced with new goals. Goals are created for your benefit and to serve your purpose. Do not develop *"tunnel vision"* and get so consumed in reaching your goal that you lose sight of whether it still holds a desired purpose.

Goals should have assigned priorities. This will help keep your attention focused on what's important and not be distracted by the unimportant, insignificant or immaterial. By prioritizing each goal you can be satisfied that their accomplishment will shape all aspects of your life that you wish to achieve.

Goals may seem to be mutually exclusive. However, if you properly balance and prioritize your personal and professional goals, they don't have to be.

Your goals should reflect what you want to achieve and not what may be the goals of your parents, spouse, family, employer or anyone else. Your goals should be your goals.

Now, let's get specific.

Goals are established from a need or desire and are then a conscious self recognition or decision that something must change.

Establishing goals makes you determine and stay focused on what is important in your life and separate it from and not be distracted by what is irrelevant.

What happens if you lose focus of your goal?

October 25, 1964, Jim Marshall, a Minnesota Vikings defensive end, recovers a fumble and runs 66 yards to the end zone. Unfortunately, it was the wrong goal, scoring for the opposing team.

I suggest that your first, foremost and one permanent goal be:

There are no failures. Always learn from whatever you achieve and use those results and lessons towards future goal-setting.

When establishing realistic effective well planned goals, consider the following guideline:

Make goals positive. "I am going to nail this interview!" Is much better than, "I hope I don't say anything stupid and blow it."

Make realistic, achievable goals. To sustain motivation and realize successful achievement, goals must be realistic and achievable. You must always believe that your goal is possible and can be accomplished (self-efficacy).

Be as detailed and precise in defining your goals as possible. Make Well Planned Goals. There is a direct relationship between how detailed and well planned your goal is and the likelihood of its favorable outcome.

Set some timetables. Set short-term and long-term timetables or time lines. Write or list them out like a project list that must be completed.

Prioritize your goals. With multiple goals, by prioritizing you can avoid becoming overwhelmed and conflicted.

Don't make conflicting goals. Review all goals to make sure that one does not conflict with another. If you set a goal to work every waking minute to get ahead in business, your goal may be in conflict with being a good and attentive spouse and parent.

Set lesser, incrementally stepped goals that lead to your larger goals. You will realize more reward from successfully completing the smaller goals, thus reinforcing your commitment and progress towards achieving the larger goal.

Base your goals on personal performance. Set goals based upon your own personal performance. You do not want to fail in achieving your goal due to injury, weather, negative business environment or other's actions, etc.

Avoid easy goals. Easy goals are set by lazy people that simply want to avoid failure or achieve superficial success.

Accurately communicate your goals to others. Make sure that others, whose actions have a direct impact on your goal achievement, clearly understand what your goal is and when or if that goal changes.

Dennis Lee, academic advisor to the STARS program established to help at-risk students, teaches two goal setting techniques. First, all goals should be **SMART**: **S**pecific, **M**easurable, **A**ction-oriented, **R**ealistic and **T**ime specific. Second, goals should satisfy **the six P's**: **P**ositive, **P**resent tense, **P**ersonal, **P**recise, **P**ossible and **P**owerful.

Goals should be positive and not involve immoral or illegal actions, created by poor judgment, vengeance or times of extreme emotions. Such goals are self destructive and counter productive. *"That guy cut me off in traffic so I'm going to speed up so I can pass and cut in front of him."* Such a goal could result in a speeding ticket, an injurious accident to you or others, costly vehicle damage, or even death. The other person could be mentally unstable or under extreme pressure or high emotions and have a weapon. No good can come from pursuit of this goal.

David C. McClelland's work, Human Motivation, differentiates three types of goals. *Mastery Goals* or learning goals that deals with achieving skills or acquiring knowledge, *Performance Goals* that deal with achievement and outperforming others, and *Social Goals* which deal with personal relationships.

The study determined that in order to achieve life success, it is critical that you have all three goals. Develop and focus your goals in each area. The failure in any one area will ultimately create overall failure.

In his book, Albert Bandura, Social Foundations of Thought and Action: A Social-Cognitive Theory, established that you must have both self-efficacy and self-regulation.

Self-Efficacy is the belief that an action (or goal) is possible and can be accomplished.

Self-Regulation is the establishment of goals, developing and committing to a plan to attain the goals, reviewing results and modifying if necessary.

As we discussed in the chapter dealing with self motivation and commitment, an important factor for motivation is to have a high degree of value associated with the successful achievement of your goal. Your goals need to reflect and define that high value.

Once you have all your goals detailed and defined, you must

develop your plans to reach those goals.

We all would prefer to spend time doing rather than thinking. However, if you don't take time to think about where you are going, how are you going to get there?

Often the time taken to do a job correctly is only invested after the job was done wrong as a result of not taking the time to plan it right in the beginning. Investing time in the planning process in advance will result in the more efficient and productive utilization of time and resources which will be rewarded with the successful achievement of your goal.

You may be familiar with the Pareto Principle. With planning, this principle relates to 80% of the productive work is accomplished in 20% of the time applied. The non-planning approach then would be that only 20% of the productive work is accomplished in 80% of the time applied. The rest probably will not be accomplished.

This principle relates to the importance of effective front end and continuous planning.

So, let's take some time to understand how to properly plan.

There are two types of planning, strategic and operational. Strategic planning is less specific, longer term, visionary and conceptual, dealing with where you are ultimately going. Operational planning is shorter term, specific in action, with desired, identifiable and measurable results and addresses how you are going to get there.

Operational planning is today and tomorrow.

As George L. Morrisey states in his book *Creating Your Future: Personal Strategic Planning for Professionals,* do not adopt any pre-prepared or packaged planning system. Your plan should be designed around your own specific knowledge, experiences, time, resources and personality.

Look to the future. Your plan should stay focused on today, tomorrow and future goals and not get distracted or derailed by the past. All plans are a map to a future point of completion.

Well thought out. Plans should be detailed and thought out identifying all alternatives, possibilities and contingencies that you can consider and anticipate. Your response to something that has a significant impact to your plan will be more favorably effective if you have already considered it in advance. It is always better to act than it is to react.

Constant review. Reviewing plans for change or modification is inevitable. The difficulty is to recognize when a plan needs revision based upon changing circumstances.

Complacency. During good times, we all would like to think that it will continue forever. It won't. Planning is usually needed as much as ever to avoid obstacles that would send us in an unfavorable direction.

Avoiding crisis. If you are constantly enduring crisis situations, you probably are a victim of the lack of proper planning or ineffective planning.

Communication. Plans that require the participation of others must be properly communicated to those that may have an impact to its successful outcome.

As with goal setting, writing down or listing your plans can be very constructive towards disciplining yourself for effective completion.

Timetables and deadlines can be internal or external. Internal is established totally within yourself. These are, unfortunately, easier to break, fail, forget or extend. External timetables or deadlines are established with others or because of others and are more likely to be kept.

For example, an internal timetable may be to leave by a specific time for Orlando. You may set a time but it can easily slide forward or backward. An external timetable would be that you must catch a plane for Orlando that leaves at 4:00 pm. That would be either kept or missed.

Recognize and understand why people fail to properly plan.

> *Being active instead of thoughtful.* Human nature is that we want to act instead of taking time to think. Considered thought directs effective activity.

> *Make your goals yours.* Failure is almost certain when trying to achieve the goals others have set or expect for you. No one else can set your goals and no one else can achieve them. It's up to you alone.

> *Laziness.* Many people are simply lazy.

> *Lack of vision or insight.* Some cannot see the benefits to planning, feel no need to plan, or may not recognize that things need to change.

> *Fear of failure.* Many people simply are so afraid to fail that they choose to take no action at all, thus not failing.

> *Experience.* Someone that repeats the same thing, may feel that their previous experience negates the need for planning. Forethought is a trait of professionalism and the predecessor of success.

Poor reward goals. Some within business may feel it better to do nothing than take a risk and fail when there is little or no value to be received.

Crisis control. If your time or life is deeply consumed with crisis', you obviously don't take time to plan.

Previous poor planning. When there was previous planning, if the plan was cumbersome, complex, confusing, poorly conceived, poorly communicated and completed with bad results or failed altogether.

Stuck in a rut. Many people are simply stuck in their routine and unable or do not desire to seek positive and constructive planning.

Strategic planning is long-term, visionary and evolves with changing desires, needs and circumstances.

Strategic planning must also be constantly reviewed and updated to reflect changes and to maintain focus for more current operational goals. Your operational (short-term) goals must always be consistent with your strategic (long-term) goals.

Goals can be initially achieved but ultimately fail from poor planning or lack of planning.

Jeremy saves money for years and finally achieves goal of opening his own hair stylist shop equipped with the best products, chairs and accessories. He files business and personal bankruptcy after four months. Jeremy had spent all of his savings and financing on the shop furnishings and supplies while providing for no working capital. Everything he owned was financed and there was no other source of income or borrowing. Jeremy had failed to plan for the necessary working capital to carry his business and provide the time to establish a profitable clientele. After years of saving, Kimberly is in the position to open her own business. Her background is in personal care and spa services. Kimberly does not spend the proper time to decide, plan and identify what her specific business purpose will be and her targeted customer. Her choices were: hair salon, nail salon, tanning salon, facial care, spa treatment, etc. She spends time and money on the location and equipment only to change her targeted services and clientele as employees are hired with varying qualifications and experience. However, Kimberly kept changing the identity of the business costing her time and money changing equipment and remodeling the shop. The business was failing and unprofitable because she never invested the time to plan, focus and stay focused on a business purpose and direction. No marketing plan was ever developed, she could not stay identified on what her services were. She had established the goal of opening a business but had failed to invest time on planning.

Successful people have a common foundation. Either by recognition, education, training or instinct, they started early to establish achievable goals. In the beginning they may have been small, short-term and achievable without a large degree of effort however, this created a habit or protocol that they diligently follow with unwavering discipline in their personal and professional lives.

One very successful person used the following analogy.

Imagine your goal as the bull's-eye on a dart board. You have a very narrow margin of variance in throwing the dart and still hitting the bulls-eye. That margin of variance represents how much you can be distracted from or compromise your plans and still successfully reach your goal and hit the bulls-eye. If you vary outside that margin, you will miss the bulls-eye and only achieve some lesser score, or result.

Allen Questrom, described as the most prolific corporate turn-around artist in the United States, at a University of Florida symposium stated that the one common problem of all the failed companies he was brought in to fix was, *"... They had lost focus ... They forgot what they stood for."* In summary, he brought each company back to focus on the few goals it needed and eliminated anything that distracted time from or did not support those goals.

The lesson we can learn is that we all can easily find our focus and what we stand for.

If you are not practiced with goal setting and planning, begin training yourself by establishing smaller short-term goals and preparing related plans for achieving those goals.

Analyze and learn from your results (remembering the number one goal *"There are no failures"*). See what worked and why and what did not work and why. This will better train and prepare you for your future planning and goal setting.

Once you have accomplished some *"training"* goals and planning, your goals can become more sophisticated and complex with experience and inner phased with strategic (long-term) goals.

The characteristics of a successful person are those that permit them to establish realistic well defined achievable goals. They are able to properly develop and implement plans in achieving those goals and communicating those goals and plans to others whose actions have an impact to them.

GOALS

1. *There are no failures,* only learning opportunities.
2. *Make each goal a positive.*
3. *Goals are to be realistically achievable.*
4. *Make your goals yours,* not those of others.
5. *Be as specific and detailed as possible.*
6. *Create written timetables or timelines.*
7. *Prioritize your goals.*
8. *Don't make conflicting goals.*
9. *Use smaller goals* working towards larger goals.
10. *Base goals upon personal performance.*
11. *Avoid easy goals for superficial success.*
12. *Life success* depends upon having Mastery Goals, Performance Goals and Social Goals.
13. *You must believe goals to be possible.*
    Develop and commit to a plan that is subject to modification.
14. *Communicate your goals effectively* to those whose actions directly impact them.

PLANS

1. *Strategic planning* is visionary and long-term.
2. *Operational planning* is short-term, specific and takes action.
3. *Invest time* in the planning process.
4. *Tailor your own personal plan* to fit your attributes.
5. *Focus your plan to the future.*
6. *Make plans as detailed and thought out as possible,* considering all alternatives, possibilities and considered contingencies.
7. *Constantly review plan* for changes or modifications.
8. *Do not become complacent* with success.
9. *Avoid crisis* from inadequate planning.
10. *Communicate plans and goals* to all that may impact results.

THE BOTTOM LINE

Developing goals is fairly easy and even often instinctive. The degree of successful achievement of those goals will be directly proportional to the amount of disciplined time spent planning, defining, reviewing and revising those goals. As the situation, conditions and goals themselves change and evolve, that advance investment of time and planning will prepare you for action instead of reaction. You must always stay focused on those goals.

A thoughtful response is always better than a thoughtless reaction.

A. Answer to previous chapter question.

"My friend Harry and I are saving up money

for a pet store. I got worms!"

Dumb and Dumber

CHAPTER TWENTY-TWO

Thinking Ahead

"Yesterday is not ours to recover, but tomorrow is ours to win or lose."
— Former President, Lyndon B. Johnson

WEBSTER'S
"To have or formulate in the mind in advance."

MINE
*"To visualize forward and match current actions or
decisions with considered future needs or desired results."*

Thinking ahead is an important learned trait of successful people, being able to look forward, considering different options, actions, scenarios, tactics, outcomes and changes. Being prepared to make a considered, anticipated, prepared or informed action or reaction to events as life simply happens.

According to a recent study by The Corporate Strategy Board, about one-third of all major American Companies engage in *"Scenario Planning"*.

You may not have heard of the position of Vice President of Strategy. You will more and more as other Companies realize Scenario Planning identifies possible outcomes and allows them to be positioned and prepared for problems or opportunities when others are caught by surprise and get left behind because they never saw it coming.

Scenario Planning involves Flexible Planning. Considering possible outcomes, changes, problems, etc., and having a considered scenario for each action you can identify. Being flexible to adjust your plans for changes that develop, whether you anticipated them or not.

There is usually one thing that will trigger Scenario Planning. One element that will be the catalyst for your thinking of how something impacts your plans and what changes you need to make in response, if any. For example, you receive that promotion that requires you to move to a different state or an unexpected pregnancy, a divorce, death, winning the lottery, losing your job, an injury requiring retirement.

Consider most games or sports. They usually involve Scenario Planning and Flexible Planning. Skill games require strategies and tactics. Chance games involve risk taking.

In football, there are specific plans for third and long, different from second and short. There are plans for player injuries. There are early game plans and late game plans. All of these plans utilize Scenario and Flexible Planning.

The game of chess is an excellent example. Chess is about thinking ahead and anticipating outcomes and related responses. Planning your future moves, anticipating your opponents possible responses to those moves and then your following move based upon each possible response.

Great chess players are those that practice, practice, practice, studying past games and learning from all that practicing and studying.

The analogy of games and sports to life only fails in that games and sports have specific, definable and finite rules. Life more often than not, doesn't. As has been advised by those with a military background, don't get caught up in the minutia of the details or the complexity of the situation to the extent that you lose sight of the victory.

Think *"outside the box"*.

Successful people are able to see through or past the limitations that create roadblocks for others. They become able to exploit opportunities by seeing beyond life's limitless defined and undefined rules without breaking them.

There are three periods in life. Past, Present and Future.

Our present is a result of the decisions and choices that we made in our past. Our future will reflect the results of the decisions and choices we make in the present.

Therefore, as we live with the results of our past decisions and choices, the farther we can think and see ahead to base our current decisions and choices, the better our future will be.

History lessons increases your ability to predict future outcomes.

History teaches which strategies or tactics have worked in the past and which have failed.

History will give you an edge over others who will unknowingly be spending time trying to reinvent the wheel. (Trying to do what has failed in the past but they don't know it.)

Ask "What If?" Answering this simple question can be critical. *"**What if** you get the job and have to relocate? Can you?" "**What if** you start your new business and it is successful? Can you handle the resulting personal and family demand?"*

Thinking. If you find yourself zoning (as my kids use to call it), mindlessly going through the motions or simply staring into space, it's time to step back and start thinking again. Somehow you have been distracted.

Our life is like traveling a pathway. You can look back and see where you came from and how you got to where you are now. Most importantly, how can you see where you are going if you don't look ahead?

Over the years I have tried to impress on my daughter more than once, *"The decisions and choices you make today will affect what your life will be like tomorrow just like your life today is a result of your past decisions and choices."* When something goes wrong, have you ever asked yourself, *"Why did this happen to me?"* Was your answer destiny or s--t happens? If you are truthful it's probably because you failed to look or think about how something you did in the past would affect your future.

Thinking ahead:

A police officer pulls a guy over for speeding and has the following exchange.

Officer: *May I see your driver's license please?*

Driver: *I don't have one. I had it suspended when I got my 5th DUI.*

Officer: *May I see your registration for the vehicle?*

Driver: *It's not my car. I stole it.*

Officer: *This is a stolen car?*

Driver: *That's right. But come to think of it, I think I saw the registration in the glove box when I was putting my gun in there.*

Officer: *There's a gun in the glove box?*

Driver: *Yes sir. That's where I put it after I shot and killed the woman who owns this car and stuffed her body in the trunk.*

Officer: *There's a DEAD BODY in the TRUNK?!?!?!?*

Driver: *Yes Sir.*

Hearing this the officer immediately called his captain. The car was quickly surrounded by police, and the captain approached the driver to handle the situation.

Captain: *Sir, may I see your license?*

Driver: *Sure. Here it is. (Handing the Captain his license.)*

It was a current and valid drivers license.

Captain: *Is this your car?*

Driver: *It's mine officer. Here's the registration. (Handing it to the captain)*

The car was owned by the driver.

Captain: *Could you slowly open your glove box so I can see if there's a gun it?*

Driver: *Yes sir, but there's no gun in it.*

Sure enough, upon opening the glove box, there was no gun.

Captain: *Would you mind opening the trunk? I was told you said there's a body in it.*

Driver: *No problem.*

The trunk was opened and found to be empty.

Captain: *I don't understand it. The officer who stopped you said you told him you didn't have a license, stole the car, had a gun in the glove box and had killed a lady and put her dead body in the trunk.*

Driver: *Yea, I'll bet the lying SOB told you I was speeding too.*

(Original author unknown)

Consider the following true real life examples of innocent results from not thinking ahead:

Cheryl begins a project of painting the concrete floor of her screened back porch. She begins at the doors leading from the house and continues past the screen door opening to the outside at the same end of the porch. Cheryl painted herself into the corner of the porch without a door or window and no means of leaving until the paint dried.

Mary instructs her husband to dig up a large plant from the front yard and replant it at the side of the house where she thought it would look nice. Then she sends her husband to Home Depot to purchase the exact same plant for planting in the hole in the front yard left from the removal of the original plant. When asked, "Why didn't you just purchase the new plant and plant it on the side of the house where you wanted one instead of removing the one in your front yard and then having to replace it when you wanted the same plant?" Mary's response, "I didn't think of that."

———◦◦◦◦◦———

"A prudent man foresees the difficulties ahead and prepares for them; The simpleton goes blindly on and suffers the consequences."

—Proverbs 22:3 (TLB)

———◦◦◦◦◦———

THINKING AHEAD

1. *Knowing history helps* you predict future outcomes.
2. *History teaches strategies* and tactics that have worked and failed in the past.
3. *Historical knowledge* will give you an edge over others that will spend time reliving what didn't work.
4. *Ask "What If?"* Ask the question and examine all the answers.
5. *Think outside the box.* See possibilities that others can't or don't.
6. *Think ahead.* Consider scenarios on different decisions or choices and your alternative responses. As in chess, look as far ahead as possible for your moves, others responses and your alternatives.
7. *Practice, Practice, Practice.*

THE BOTTOM LINE

Thinking ahead requires that you first look and then practice. It will provide you an edge with games, sports, family, business, and more importantly, life events. Your past has shaped and determined your present, and your present decisions and choices will decide and determine your future. Learn from history and consider all current choices and decisions carefully, how each will affect your present and impact your future. Scenario and Flexible Planning will help you in preparing for those changes, problems, opportunities and related foreseeable possible outcomes.

Avoiding Failure

CHAPTER TWENTY-THREE

Reading Before Signing

"How can you see your future if you don't take time to look?"

— Mark C. Middleton

WEBSTER'S

*"To examine and grasp the meaning of written or
printed characters, words, or sentences."*

MINE

*"The complete review, comprehension and <u>understanding
by the person obligated to sign</u>, prior to signing."*

This is probably the single most self aware problem that I have dealt with. Everyone seems to already know of and recognize the simple concept of reading something before you sign it but so often casually and nonchalantly, don't. Later, they are upset to find out what they legally agreed and bound themselves to.

I can't even begin to count the number of times (and it would be in the hundreds if not thousands) I have dealt with people that have to face the ramifications of the documents they signed, and have responded with the only defense or explanation, *"I didn't read it"* or *"I read it but I didn't understand what it meant"* or *"I relied on (he, she or them) to have read it and explain it to me."*

Throughout our personal and business lives, we are all submitted documents for signing that we don't read or we rely on others to have read and understand. Sometimes we are not expected to read them or it is hoped that we don't read them, and in fact we do not (to the great satisfaction of the other party).

Let's consider the following partial list.

Purchasing Insurance's.	Acquiring Credit Cards.
Purchasing/Leasing a Vehicle.	Opening a Bank Account.
Opening a Brokerage Account	Purchasing or Selling a Home.
Signing a Will.	Signing a Trust.
Various Contracts.	Employment Agreements.
Professional/Personal Services.	Medical Treatment Forms.
Income Tax Returns	

A great majority of documents are preprinted, fill in the blank forms. We should all differentiate between those required by Government Authority, when applicable, and those required or preferred by the other party. Recognize that those prepared by the other party's are almost always prepared by attorneys to:

1. Satisfy disclosure requirements required by law.
2. Protect their clients interests.
3. Meet the directed purpose and instructions of their clients.
4. Limit your legal rights, recourse or recovery against their clients.

I suggest you closely scrutinize any documents required by anyone that are on company preprinted forms, contracts, agreements, disclosures, estimates, notes, purchase orders, etc.

You will discover MAA's or MAC's. Mandatory Arbitration Agreements or Mandatory Arbitration Clauses. These agreements are used by automobile dealerships, stock brokerages, Internet services, advertising outlets, credit card contracts, consumer services, cable TV, cellular telephone providers, online retailers, gyms, financing companies, travel agencies, health maintenance organizations, private doctors, credit agencies, video rentals, financial services, and the list gets longer each passing year. **THESE AGREEMENTS/CLAUSES ARE NOT REQUIRED BY LAW.**

THESE AGREEMENTS/CLAUSES ARE NOT REQUIRED BY LAW.

THEY ARE DESIRED/REQUIRED

ONLY BY THE COMPANY YOU ARE DEALING WITH.

THESE AGREEMENTS LIMIT YOUR RIGHTS

TO DAMAGES FROM OR CLAIMS

AGAINST THE COMPANY.

This is important and was worth repeating.

Some Companies give the option to back out of the clauses with a 30 day window when the arbitration contract is revised, but if you miss the opportunity, you're locked in.

There are many companies that are resisting the requirement to sign these agreements, but you really have to search for them. As of this writing, credit cards issued by AARP, some small credit unions, the wireless provider Nextel, do not require these agreements.

In my local personal experience, as an example, when shopping for a new vehicle, the local Ford and Chevrolet dealerships both required the signing of the Mandatory Arbitration Agreement and Toyota did not. Yes, my wife and I both drive Toyotas.

A Vestavia Hills, Ala. lady, when paying her monthly bill for termite control treatment and insurance, she included a note stating that by cashing the check the company was agreeing to let her out of the mandatory arbitration clause. The check was cashed and the Alabama Supreme Court ruled that her release was enforceable.

I would encourage everyone to exercise your right to not sign such agreements and if it is required by the other party, politely decline and find someone else to do business with.

Many documents are quite lengthy, printed on both sides of the paper and in small print. These obviously should be especially read and understood completely. I would also suggest that the other party presenting such document for signing be required to remain with you while you read it so that any part not understood can be thoroughly explained. This certainly may be time consuming to the extent that they will not want to, but then they should not require such documents be signed if they are not willing to spend their time to explain and assist you with understanding them. **That is their fault and not yours.**

You will discover that at many times, they also will not understand all the provisions. You should not sign that document until they can explain everything even if they must find a superior or call another office.

Pre-prepared documents often have many provisions unrelated to your individual situation. Those provisions should be struck through in the document with both parties initialing the exclusion.

An example,

> *A gentleman drives his car to the local dealership and looks at a new one. He agrees to a trade value and writes a check for the difference that was presented to him in the paperwork. Twenty four months later he receives a letter outlining his requirements for returning his leased vehicle or paying an additional amount to purchase it. He believed that he had purchased the vehicle in the beginning when in actuality he had leased it with an up front lump sum payment. The paperwork did identify it as a lease, but he had not read it before signing.*

Obviously, the additional benefit to reading documents before signing is that you will certainly be cognizant of all your restrictions, obligations and requirements, as well as theirs, and all that you are to receive. In addition, do not rely on the other party to get it right. While you are reading, you are also checking for mistakes in your name, social security number, address, telephone number, terms and conditions, what you agreed to, what they agreed to, everything.

> *Wills prepared by an attorney for a couple that signed without reading them first. During an estate planning process with a review of both of the wills, the husbands will left everything to his wife, the wife's will left everything to the husband and in the event of simultaneous deaths, everything was left to the husband. They would have easily caught this if only they had read the wills prior to signing them.*

The most difficult time to exercise your right to read before signing is when you are presented with a mountain of documents that are extensive and maybe routine to the other person but not to you. They will simply want to rush through the signature procedure, but don't. Not only read each and every document but understand it.

You are also entitled to a copy of each and every document you sign. You can keep track of the signing of multiple documents by numbering your signature on each document you sign and then checking to see that you have in fact received a copy of each signed document.

When signing multiple page documents, initial and date each page that is not a signature page to prevent any substitution or changes of pages in the future. You would like to believe that you would never deal with anyone that would do that, but the following are real life examples:

Acme, Inc. Board of Directors voted at a meeting to enter into a contract with Telstar Corporation. After approval, Telstars representative meets individually with each corporate officer of Acme and presents the signature page of the contract for signing without the body of the contract, which all seven directors sign. The original contract pages were substituted and added to the signed signature page assigning all of the assets of Acme to Telstar and liquidating Acme, Inc. Litigation is pending at this time.

US Homes prepares a complete multi-page copy of your home construction contract that is initialed and dated by both parties on each page with the last page signed by all parties. Whenever a change is made to add, change or delete anything, a complete new copy is prepared with every page of the revised contract being initialed and the last page signed. Each revised contract is clearly identified as a revision of the previous version of the original contract. This is a Company that is acting in the best interest of their customers and themselves.

Reading a document before you sign it is probably the easiest and simplest thing that you can do personally and in business. Failure to do so probably causes the costliest loss of money, time and productivity and is so easily avoided and rectified.

There should never be an obligation in any document that you were not aware of. You should be aware of everything expected from you and obligated to you from the other party. There should be no words, clauses, provisions, terms, references, terminologies, concepts, phrases, or requirements that you do not fully understand.

You should not rely solely on the other party's explanation of any of the foregoing, be satisfied even if you must obtain your own independent explanation.

You should make sure you are reading intelligently. Other than for entertainment, consider the following tips for developing good reading strategies:

Know what you are looking for. Identify in advance those terms, conditions, obligations and considerations that make up the contract or agreement. It is your responsibility to make sure they are all as you and the other party agreed to and expect.

Before beginning, think about the purpose of the document. Make sure the document is for whatever purpose you intend. The right document for the transaction.

Read sitting upright at a desk or table with good light. Avoid reading at times of fatigue, anxiety, pressure, urgency or hunger. Have the time necessary to properly commit to the reading.

Be an active reader. When reading a document in detail, highlight and underline important terms, words, sentences or paragraphs. This will help you to focus on the material and commit it to memory as well as quickly find it later for review. If an original of a document is not to be marked, make a copy that can be marked up.

Have pen and paper available for notes.

Keep background noise low if at all. Soft music, not loud or only a low television or radio, if any. No distracting children or crowd noises. Have a relaxing, quiet environment that won't be distracting. If in an office with outside distractions, close the door.

Know what to read and what can be skimmed. There is often a lot of "Boiler Plate" disclosures and language in documents that is required by government regulations. You will become familiar with identifying such sections and skim them. The sections with the "Meat" of the document should be read and understood carefully.

"Whole Subject" documents. In any important document, the writer will present a specific thought and presentation structure. This may intentionally be done to obscure important information and include irrelevant detail. If you take a minute and list out the important points, terms, agreements, etc. before beginning the document, this will function as your own table of contents that will guide you through the document and enable you to identify any important points. You will also locate and verify those points and terms in the document and match them to your list.

Translate difficult or confusing sections into your own words. Create an alternative text to explain in your own words any parts that seem confusing or unclear.

Do not engage in, what I call, **selective reading.** I would define this as reading until you think you have the information you need or the answer you wanted. Once this happens, too many people stop reading or gloss over the remaining material. In the following examples, many people will stop reading after getting the information they wanted and fail to read the bold italic portions:

For business, you may deduct the purchase of a SUV up to $102,000, *if purchased before October 23, 2004.*

You will receive a 2.5% discount on your total purchases *if your payment is made in full by the 20th of the month.*

Your deposit will be refunded in full upon return of your vehicle by *6:00 p.m.*

Your account will not be charged a monthly service charge, *as long as you maintain a minimum balance of $500.*

You may do this, *as long as you also do that.*

Practicing good reading strategies will help with any reading material to ensure better and clearer comprehension. Now that you have read and understand the document, make sure before signing that you are in complete agreement with all of the terms, conditions, agreements, representations, requirements and information contained therein. It is your responsibility and yours alone. You will live with the consequences, not the salesman, attorney, accountant, financial planner, banker, salesman, broker or anyone else.

READING BEFORE SIGNING

1. *Before signing anything, read it first.*
2. *Have the other party remain with you* while you read.
3. *Have the other party explain* and clarify anything that you do not completely understand.
4. *If you are not comfortable* that something is being properly explained, get an explanation from someone you trust.
5. *Do not leave any blanks* that are not filled in.
6. *Make sure you know all of your obligations.*
7. *Make sure there are no errors* in dollar amounts, terms, conditions, names, dates, etc.
8. *You may be able to modify any documents* that have provisions that do not apply to you.
9. *Initial and date each page that is not a signature page* when signing a multiple page document.
10. *Number each signature* to ensure that you receive a copy of everything that you signed with multiple documents.
11. *Identify those documents or disclosures required by law* as distinguished from those required by the other party and scrutinize them closely.
12. *Read completely.* Don't stop after you think you understand and have the answer you think you wanted.
13. *Avoid signing and Mandatory Arbitration Agreements (MAA's).*
14. *Get a copy of everything signed by you and/or the other party.*

GOOD READING STRATEGIES

1. *Begin a document with an open mind.* Read what it says, not what you want it to say.
2. *Know what you are looking for* in the document.
3. *Think about the purpose of the document.*
4. *Read sitting up and with good lighting.*
5. *Be an active reader.* Highlight important points.
6. *Have pen and paper ready* for making notes.
7. *Keep out all background noise* or at least minimize it.
8. *Identify what material can be scanned* and what you should read in detail.
9. *List out important points* before beginning to identify and prevent any omissions and to make sure they are included.
10. *Translate difficult or confusing sections* into your own words.

THE BOTTOM LINE

Any document you sign legally commits you to it. "I didn't read it" is no defense and does not release you from its terms, conditions and requirements. Many documents have a material affect on your future and/or the future of your business or family in terms of rights, benefits and obligations.

Begin any document with an open mind. Do not develop preconceptions that influence you to read something to say what you want it to say as opposed to what it does say. Do not read selectively.

Investing sometimes only a few minutes up front can often avoid extensive future costly time or even possible litigation and ensure that you are giving and receiving what you expected. How can you achieve Personal Success if you don't even take the time necessary to read and understand what you are committing yourself to?

CHAPTER   TWENTY-FOUR

Have It In Writing

"A verbal contract isn't worth the paper it is written on."

— Sam Goldwyn

WEBSTER'S

"To compose or set down in literary form."

MINE

"Creating a written document that: supports verbal communications, outlines details and facts, forms a record of information."

The failure of a written version of a contract, agreement, important communication, representations, terms, obligations, performances, guarantees, financial obligations or expectations, etc. can lead to lost time and productivity, cost money and, possibly more importantly, lead to irreversibly broken relationships.

It is always best to have anything important be put in writing. This obvious but simple point is violated by us all, at least at some time in life.

For example, take the case of the Cleveland Cavaliers who thought they had reached a verbal agreement with basketball great Carlos Boozer for a long term deal only to have him sign with the Utah Jazz after receiving a better offer. They did not put it in writing.

In working with successful business people, you can usually find a very well documented filing and record system. Important communications are documented with follow-up memos, E-mails or letters. Handwritten notes abound detailing telephone conversations and social contacts when something noteworthy is discussed, all recording time, date and specifics about what the other party said and what answers were given.

It is critical to have detailed notes being specific and exact as to facts presented and questions asked by someone and your exact answer. At a later time when you may be challenged on the correctness of your answer, you can make sure that no details or facts have been changed, omitted or added from the original conversation and this happens a lot in business.

Keep in mind that more often than not when an issue or problem arises, it is after some length of time has passed, memories fade (both yours and others) and people that you originally dealt with are no longer there. It is at that time you will appreciate the value of being able to produce documentation that clearly and precisely presents all of the facts, information, representations, obligations and requirements.

Often issues must be resolved by those that had no involvement in the original issue. Imagine your spouse having to deal with an issue you were involved in a couple years ago because for whatever reason you can't. Certainly you would want available to them the best possible records. In the worst case scenario, your attorney and the judge making a decision will appreciate it.

Have you ever had representations made to you by a salesperson only to later find out they were not true, correct, complete or had limitations? Often you have only what is verbally represented and what is represented in exhaustive confusing legalese detailed booklets or documents.

Consider requesting from a salesperson that any representations or warranties be written in simple and concise layman's terms that you can understand and then signed by that salesperson.

Memory is selective, a good document is explicit.

Memory is individual, writing is community.

Memory is distant and distorting,
the written word is a retrievable record.

There will be times that you will be unable to receive a written version of details, answers or representations when requested from the other party following an important conversation. It is to your benefit to initiate contact with them in writing, presenting your understanding of any and all important details, representations, arrangements, etc. being specific and thereby shifting the burden of any disagreement to the other party. If they do not respond, you still won't have anything in writing from them, however, you will now have supportive evidence of the points that they will have agreed to by their failure to respond, correct or challenge.

Always remember that when you are writing a communication, make sure you construct it clearly, correctly and to your benefit. Address the salient points and avoid being overly narrative or wordy. Although not all documents are contracts, all documents will produce evidence, either for you or against you. As is known to attorneys, the E in E-mail is short for EVIDENCE.

You will deal with people that do not want to put something in writing, much less sign it. They may feel that this represents a lack of trust. The experienced and honest person will not have a problem with a written statement or agreement or be insulted, most likely viewing a request for a written statement as an indication of professionalism.

Creating a written and signed agreement is most uncomfortable when dealing with family, relatives or close friends. However, keep in mind that many family and friends become estranged after differing expectations or broken perceived understandings because of unwritten agreements.

A young professional agrees to have lunch with the President of a rival firm. The President verbally offers him a partnership position with salary, bonus and benefits. They shake hands agreeing to meet later and return to the company where the young professional is introduced to all of the staff as a new partner. The next day the young professional calls the President to schedule a follow up meeting and leaves a message. Over the next several days he calls and leaves more messages. Finally he is told by the receptionist that the President has sold the company and the partnership position no longer exists. The young professional never hears from the President again. He could have prepared, at least, a hand written letter of intent to be signed by both parties at lunch.

A couple selling their home meets with a prospective buyer. After much discussion, offer and counteroffers, they arrive at an agreed sales/purchase amount and terms. They shake hands and agree to meet the next day. Buyer is never heard from again. Seller should have required offer be made with written contract before engaging in extensive negotiation.

A business owner that is selling his company talks with his accountant for some tax planning. The owner has his attorney fax sales information to the accountant afterwards for additional three way discussion. When the sale is completed, the accountant discovered that important specific details of the sale had been omitted by the owner and the attorney. Fortunately, the accountant had kept detailed notes of the meeting referencing what was said by who and also the attorney's fax. The accountant followed up with a letter to the owner outlining omitted details that would have had an impact on the prior tax planning discussions and answers.

A professional meets with an upset client business owner and his secretary. The secretary represented that she had left several telephone messages to the professional on behalf of the owner without receiving a return call. The professional's office fortunately had an answering system that logs all incoming telephone numbers. With the retrieval of those records, he established that no calls had been received from the secretary or the company during the time period claimed. Faced with this information, the secretary acknowledged to the owner that she had failed to place the calls.

HAVE IT IN WRITING

1. *Put anything important in writing.*
2. *Write letters,* notes or E-mail's to document important conversations.
3. *Be clear,* concise and specific.
4. *Note all facts and details* presented and be specific as to any answers you provide.
5. *All documents produce evidence,* either for you or against you.
6. *Written agreements establish professionalism.*

THE BOTTOM LINE

Anything important should be put in writing and when possible, signed by all pertinent parties. If you cannot get the other person to sign, then document in writing your understanding with them by letter or E-mail. Keep notes and files of all contacts and conversations. Being able to prove the facts of the conversations, requirements, conditions and representations of yours and the other parties with written documents is the difference between being a winner or a loser.

CHAPTER TWENTY-FIVE

Financial Waste

"How many things can I do without!"

— Socrates

WEBSTER'S

"The management of money, banking, investments, and credit.
To use, consume, or expend carelessly or thoughtlessly."

MINE

"The needless loss of income, erosion of assets or
existence of unnecessary expense or cost."

You knew that there had to be at least part of a book written by an accountant dealing with finances, savings, planning and wealth accumulation.

All to often the accumulation of personal wealth is hindered by avoidable Financial Waste.

We all set financial goals such as the purchase of a new car, to save for your children's college education, purchase your own home, save for retirement, etc. Certainly wouldn't it be great to be able to afford those things sooner? Wouldn't it be great to be able to afford an even better car, bigger and/or nicer home, send your children to a better college or retire earlier?

A CASE STUDY

Daughter and son-in-law of good client asked that I assist the young, financially struggling couple with baby that were unable to make ends meet on their two incomes. We reviewed the following areas of savings.

Charge Cards can have interest rates in excess of 20%. We applied for and received a charge card that had a 0% one year introductory rate. We transferred all balances to this card and established a payment schedule to pay this off within that time. We reviewed all charge cards and canceled any that had annual fees that the issuer would not waive. In addition, I cautioned the couple to closely review every monthly statement for any charges that were not approved. We found an $8.95 monthly charge for credit protection that they were not aware of, and promptly canceled. For the future, they were counseled to only charge what was needed and could be paid off in total with the statement, never carrying a balance and, therefore, not paying interest.

Late Charges. Making late payments not only can and does incur additional charges or fees and/or interest, it can affect your credit and credit rating which will affect your interest rate on future borrowings, auto loans, mortgages, etc.

Bank Service Charges and NSF Fees. Banks are very competitive to get and keep your banking relationship. You can easily get accounts with no monthly charges, find them. Obviously, NSF (Non Sufficient Funds) charges are easily avoided by simply not writing checks if you do not have sufficient funds to cover the checks.

Account Fees. Different accounts may carry fees or charges. Make sure you review your brokerage and investment accounts, insurance policies like whole life, utility accounts, charge cards, any and all accounts for fees. When possible, get them removed or find another account that has a smaller or no fee.

ATM Fees. The fees charged by the Automated Teller Machines by most banks are avoidable by simply not using them except, perhaps, in emergencies or possibly when traveling. This couple was paying ATM fees at the monthly rate of $30-$40 per month.

Unused or Unneeded Services or Products. When you purchase a new vehicle, often roadside assistance is included with that vehicle at no additional charge for one to three years. If you also are a member of AAA with an annual fee, this is mostly a duplication of services. Monthly Credit Card Protection charges normally provide little or no additional protection than you already have by state and federal law and as a built in service of the issuing charge card.

Cellular telephone upgrades for unused services such as Internet connection, instant text messaging, Internet downloads. Automobile emergency connection services like General Motors on-star service may not be necessary for you.

Subscriptions to newspapers, magazines or other publications that you don't read or perhaps only give a short cursory review upon receipt before throwing them away are a waste of money. Internet Service Providers (ISP) charges if you don't use the Internet anymore. Video rentals by mail or any service or product not needed or used is simply throwing money away.

Mortgage Life Insurance. When they purchased their home, the lender required mortgage life insurance. This form of life insurance is expensive. We contacted the lender and confirmed that they currently qualified to cancel the coverage.

Insurance Needs. We reviewed insurance coverage's to make sure they matched their needs. We changed automobile deductibles and limits and reduced the annual premium on both of their vehicles.

Impulse Purchases. See chapter on *"Impulse Decisions."* Take time to make considered and informed purchases or investments. Quick decisions caused by emotions or trained salespeople are usually regretted, costly and a waste.

During the emotions of the moment, you easily think of and focus on all the reasons you want something or *"need"* something, the flashy car, motorcycle, expensive outfit or latest electronic whatever. More often than not, if you give yourself a day to consider it, you will then and usually only then, realize all the reasons you shouldn't make that purchase. Make purchases based upon need and not want and make sure you are honest about the need.

In the end, the amount saved by making a few changes and becoming aware equaled a savings of about 8% (about $2,800) of their annual household income. And that 8% was tax free income (savings).

Other areas to review for financial waste.

Non Productive or Under Productive Assets. If you carry a significant balance in a low or no interest account (i.e. checking) transfer excess funds for investment into a money market or certificate of deposit.   Review your investments, stocks and bonds, and measure there performance. If they are not providing a reasonable return either in interest, dividend or appreciation, find better investments.

Leasing versus Purchasing. In general, it is always better to purchase instead of lease. The overall cost (particularly with vehicles) is less to purchase and you normally have more negotiating options.

Extended Warranties and Maintenance Contracts are generally a bad idea. The average profit to those that sell/ provide those warranties or contracts is 50%.

Company Specific Charges. Many Company's have charges: Dealer Preparation, Processing, Shipping, Handling, Origination, Transfer, etc., these charges should at the very least be negotiated if not totally removed. These are distinguished separate from required governmental fees. The higher the cost of the product or service, the easier it is to include costs which can become virtually unnoticeable with the large amounts. Ever purchase a vehicle for $30,000 including sales tax only to be presented with a purchase statement that is several hundreds of dollars more? Ever purchase a home for $200,000 that requires payment and mortgage for, say $210,000? Check out each of those charges and fees. Are they government required or Company specific? Negotiate.

Comparison Shopping. Do you purchase a vehicle from the first dealership you go to? If you had gone to two or more dealerships and negotiated their best deals, you would be negotiating a purchase price from a knowledgeable position of power. This will work with electronics, furniture, many tangible consumer products. You can save by comparison shopping for airline tickets, cruise tickets, rental cars, hotels, etc.

Do you purchase automobile or homeowners insurance without getting comparison prices from several Companies? Most people will remain with their insurance Company for years, automatically renewing their coverage. Find the best deal up front, and then re-shop the coverage with other Companies every anniversary before renewing.

Some life truism's:

Discount department stores don't always have the best price.
Discount department stores don't always have the freshest
    perishables.
Discount department stores often sell outdated
    products/technology.
Name brands cost more for a reason:

Made better, works better.

Better technology.

Lasts longer than the warranty.

Buying in bulk is not always less expensive or better.

Any Negotiable Charge. Always identify and understand any and all charges. You may very well be able to negotiate many charges and fees, even with professionals which are often accepted, not questioned and paid. You never know until you try.

Unauthorized charges. Always review billing statements. Charge cards, telephone bills, medical statements, etc. You will probably discover unauthorized charges every year that can add substantially to your expenses. In my own experience, I have found several hundred dollars per year of unauthorized and/or erroneous charges.

Debt Management and Credit History. Having too much credit or high monthly payments as a percentage of your income can damage your credit rating thus affecting your ability to get the best possible terms on debt when needed (notice I said NEEDED and not WANTED). Applying too often for credit can damage your credit rating. Late payments, missed payments, negotiated settlements and bankruptcy will all damage your credit rating.

While consulting with a small business, the original engagement was to review a business, marketing and growth plan, and to identify areas to improve the sagging bottom line. Upon financial review, we discovered that Federal and State penalties and interest for the prior year totaled in the low five figures. The bottom line was significantly improved merely with the timely payments for various taxes and timely filing of related forms and returns.

A senior conservative couple had significant money on deposit in non-interest and low interest bearing checking accounts (multiple accounts with a total in excess of a million dollars). They were greatly adverse to risk. We reviewed their checking balance needs and invested excess funds in multiple Certificates of Deposit with a stepped structure (smaller amounts with varying maturities). This simple process greatly increased their income and protected their investment during a time of rising interest rates.

FINANCIAL WASTE

1. *Account fees* charged by banks, charge cards, brokerage and others should be waived or find a new company.
2. *Avoid late charges, penalties and interest.* Make payments and file reports timely.
3. *Avoid ATM machines* and fees.
4. *Unused or unneeded services and/or products* should be canceled and avoided.
5. *Non productive or under productive assets* should be converted to optimal productivity.
6. *Company charges or fees* should be negotiated to reduce or eliminate them.
7. *Comparison shopping* for products or services should be done on a continuing basis.
8. *Many charges are negotiable.* Nothing ventured, nothing gained.
9. *Debt management* should minimize debt and maximize terms.
10. *Your credit history* affects your credit rating and future credit terms.
11. *Impulse decisions* can be costly. Make any purchase or investment an informed and considered decision.

THE BOTTOM LINE

Most of us have financial waste. We are so busy trying to make a living that we just don't take the time or pay attention to our accounts, investments or lifestyles, and fail to distinguish between needs and wants. Successful people make money and generate wealth simply by better management of what they already have and will have.

CHAPTER TWENTY-SIX

Unnecessary Risks

"I compensate for big risks by always doing my homework and being well-prepared. I can take on larger risks by reducing the overall risk."

— Donna E. Shalala

WEBSTER'S
"Needless possibility of suffering harm or loss."

MINE
"Avoidable exposure to possible damage, injury, loss or liabilities."

There have been many people, successful and otherwise, that have been financially and emotionally devastated after losses, damages or injuries caused by taking, having or incurring unnecessary and avoidable risks.

This is different from, for example, necessary risks taken by investing in a start up company, opening your own business or marketing a new product.

Unnecessary risks are those taken by people, often to take short cuts, motivated by greed, negligence, ignorance or indifference. Risks caused by actions taken solely for expediency, expected productivity or economics of the moment. Unnecessary risks may be known but also include those risks that an individual may not be aware of or realize their existence, implications or presence.

As you have probably noticed, no one sues for a few thousand dollars anymore. Lawsuits are usually filed for millions. Also, wrongdoing and/or exposure can result in criminal charges followed by imprisonment.

During my practice, we developed a Risk Assessment And Prevention program. The RAAP program (we accountants love acronyms) was designed for individuals and businesses to provide a thorough review to identify areas of risks, especially those that are avoidable and determine what actions could be taken to prevent, eliminate or at least minimize those risks and protect the client from that exposure.

This program was managed by a Certified Public Accountant and utilized the independent work of various attorneys, insurance professionals, investment consultants and retirement planners. Because of the differing areas of expertise needed for differing circumstances and clients, when necessary, other professionals would be brought in as needed, i.e., computer programmers/specialists, engineers, safety experts, industry specialists, etc. All engagements were tailored to meet the clients specific situation.

Obviously the goal is to best protect the individual from damages, expensive litigation and possible judgment.

As an example, suppose a wealthy individual with an unincorporated hair stylist salon business were the client. We would examine both the individual and the Company. Certainly one of the first recommendations to best limit personal liability exposure would be to form a Corporation for the business. And there are alternatives like a Limited Liability Company (LLC) that we would discuss the pros and cons.

For the Corporation, the following examples of areas examined present a lengthy presentation merely to show to what lengths we would go.

Business Plans.

All contracts and lease agreements.

All financing agreements.

Signatures and titles (personally or officer) on all documents.

Insurance's – Liability, Medical, Vehicle, Property, Umbrella, etc. – deductibles, coverage's, etc.

Regulatory requirements – Chemical usage and/or disposal

Shop safety features – equipment, displays, flooring, electrical, child safety.

Security alarm or camera systems.

Signage

Employee qualifications and required credentials and current licenses.

Employee background checks including social security number verification. The sale of fake social security numbers and cards is a big business)

Timely payroll reporting requirements.

Workers Compensation coverage and policy.

Federal, State, County and City reporting and inspections requirements.

OSHA requirements.

Computer programs and Credit Card processing procedures and protections.

External accessibility of computer(s) and safeguards.

Ownership/Titles/Deeds of any Real Estate, vehicles and valuable equipment.

All Services provided by outside professionals and their qualifications.

Financial Reporting to Officers, Directors and Stockholders. Financial and Operational controls.

Timely filing of all tax and reporting returns.

Major suppliers, distributors or manufacturers.

If any importing or exporting, host of other issues.

Corporation requirements:

Federal, State and City filing and reporting requirements

Corporation Board of Directors minutes of meetings

Officer Compensation

Clear disclosure of business name as Corporation:

Corporation letterhead, business cards, signage, checking account, all forms, advertising and paperwork.

Officer, Director and key personnel personal activities, interests and medical history.

Provide education and training to all officers and directors.

For the individual, examples of areas to examine:

Insurance's – Life, umbrella, homeowners, vehicle, medical, disability, etc.

Titles and Deeds – How assets are titled.

Debt – Mortgages, notes, vehicle loans, charge cards, etc.

Investments

Wills and Trusts

Retirement Plans

How accounts are titled – Individual, jointly, Tenants by the Entirety, Joint Tenants With Right of Survival, etc.

Marital status and stability.

Estate Planning – Heirs and beneficiaries.

State of residency.

Kind and location of real estate other than personal residence.

Personal and Family medical history.

Personal lifestyle and hobbies.

Reviews evolved as information is gathered. For example, someone that owns a second home in Vail, Colorado and uses it exclusively for themselves is less problematic than someone that owns it and rents it out part of the year to others.

With a golf course client, for example, in addition to the obvious, we would review golf cart maintenance procedures. Poorly maintained brakes have caused unnecessary injuries and litigation. Course maintenance is reviewed for proper herbicide and pesticide applications and personnel qualifications. We would review the course proximity to water and types of water bodies. Streams and lakes requirements are different from drainage and retention areas. We would check the course proximity to other private property for pesticide, herbicide and fertilizer runoff and spray application that is naturally airborne. There are state notification, reporting and treatment laws and requirements related to hyper sensitive individuals and most golf courses have residential housing lots that adjoin it. Expensive litigation is easily avoided with awareness. The golf course and driving range layout is reviewed for exposure to individuals, adjacent highways, parking, buildings, homes and fairways. Being struck by a golf ball can: dent cars, break windows, cause injury and even kill.

This lengthy discussion, details and examples are for the purpose of providing an awareness of areas of risk that may go unnoticed or you may be unaware of.

Everything has an impact upon risk exposure and possible loss or litigation, personal liability protection, bankruptcy, judgments, divorce, death, insurance coverage's. How assets are titled, legal title and protections of money, investments and properties.

Any and all possible foreseeable areas of risk are identified with a planned response to eliminate, minimize or prepare for, protect and insulate the client against such risk.

In general, successful people are much more sensitive to and better at being aware of and defining areas of risk and, therefore, eliminate, reduce and protect themselves accordingly.

Some examples:

John & Mary, a wealthy couple, Mary is in a coma following a serious injury and is kept alive artificially. Without a living will and durable power of attorney for health care, their personal financial assets were soon exhausted leaving John broke and Mary a dependent of the State. As part of an estate plan, they both should have signed the proper powers of attorney.

A man buys a car for his girlfriend. The title was held in his name. The girlfriend causes and gets into a critical accident. The girlfriend was sued as the driver and the man was sued (in excess of insurance coverage) because the auto was titled in his name. The man should have titled the vehicle into his girlfriends name and filed as lien holder.

An individual was working at a store and was paid by check or cash but not as an employee. He injures him self and files for a Worker's Compensation Insurance claim. He naturally discovers that there is no insurance coverage and he files a complaint. The business is investigated by Worker's Compensation, State Unemployment and the Internal Revenue Service. Following audits, the business was charged for four years back premiums, employment taxes with penalties and interest. It cost the company a great deal more than the small amount they initially saved in payroll taxes and insurance.

A pesticide company utilizes unlicensed and untrained individuals for their pesticide application. After misapplication, the company is sued by the homeowners for resulting medical problems that would affect the rest of their lives and were awarded a substantial amount. By using unlicensed and untrained employees, in addition to physically injuring the homeowners, it cost them a great deal financially.

A lawn service company hires illegal immigrants to work for cash. They were raided and investigated by the Immigration and Naturalization Service. Surprisingly, although heavily fined they did not go out of business.

Harold and Ellen, a retired couple, own their home with no mortgage. Because homeowner's insurance rates have dramatically increased, they decide not to purchase insurance. Unfortunately, their home burns down at a total loss.

A successful large international corporation President sets up a subsidiary shell corporation to protect the parent Corporation and contracts to purchase some new expensive equipment for sale and distribution from a manufacturer. Unfortunately, the President signs the contract as President of the parent corporation instead of as President of the subsidiary corporation. Upon the failure to sell the equipment, the parent corporation has to pay a $2 Million settlement to cancel the contract. The President, in addition to other precautions, clearly should have signed as an officer of the subsidiary corporation.

A business individual is running late for a meeting. He exceeds the speed limit in an attempt to make up time. He causes a car accident and is disabled for life.

Following that "One for the road" drink, a now drunk driver hits a car on the way home. He suffers total financial loss, jail time and two innocent people were injured, one critically changing the rest of all their lives.

Consider some of the following tips in making a self-assessment of your own situation and the possible existence of Unnecessary Risks.

Are you an owner in a business? If so, are you personally insulated from litigation if something goes wrong?

Are you an officer or director of a Corporation? If so, are you personally insulated from litigation if something goes wrong?

Are you the legal titled or deeded owner of property used and controlled by another? An example is a vehicle, real estate, handgun, credit card.

Are you taking short cuts for expediency, production or profit? Paying someone *"off the books"*, substituting sub-standard product, doing a job that you think is *"good enough"* instead of correct, getting by without sufficient staff, using unqualified people. Are you doing your job with less attention to quality because of work demands or delaying or ignoring automobile maintenance, avoiding medical checkups?

Do you have the proper insurance's, limits and coverage? Life, homeowners, medical, disability, automobile, umbrella, renters.

Are your money and investment accounts titled for best protection? Individual, joint, JTWROS, Tenancy in the Entirety, etc.

Are your business relations honest and reputable? Do you associate with honest and moral or dishonest and amoral people? Know who you are dealing with and don't fool yourself into thinking their dealings with you will be any different from who they are and how they behave.

A bunny and a poisonous scorpion, escaping a forest fire, met at the edge of a creek while the fire started to surround them. The scorpion, looking across the creek to the shore, said to the bunny, *"I can't swim. I will perish in the fire."* The bunny knew the scorpion was deadly, but taking pity, the bunny said *"Climb onto my back and I will swim us both across the creek to safety."* The scorpion climbed up onto the bunny and they entered the water. The scorpion stayed dry and safe on the back of the bunny as he swam. About halfway across the water, the scorpion stung the bunny. With great surprise and disbelief the bunny said to the scorpion, *"Now we will both drown. Why did you sting me?"* The scorpion replied, *"Because that is my nature."*

Jane has a history of bad debt and poor personal financial management. She often has bill collectors calling her or seeking her out. She approaches Debbie, a small office owner, to rent office space. Debbie is aware of Jane's history but, since she is a nice person, rents the space to Jane. After about six months, slow rent payments and being behind a couple months, Jane packs up her supplies one evening and leaves without returning or contacting Debbie. In addition, Jane had incurred several unpaid expenses for office supplies, telephone and others. After non-payment, those companies approached Debbie, since Jane had worked out of her facility, they associated her with Debbie. The actions of Jane cost Debbie financially and in reputation in the business community.

For whatever reason, Debbie believed that Jane would not do to her what she had done to so many others. Debbie thought Jane would be different. Debbie failed to realize that Jane would continue to behave according to her nature.

Over the years in our practice we declined or terminated many clients for various reasons. There are five that left a lasting impression. Two of them the owners were eventually arrested and went to jail for criminal actions. One closed because of shoddy work product and reputation. The other two I simply lost track of.

We were particularly happy that our accounting firm was not included in the newspapers related to or associated with these Companies. Our internal Client Risk Evaluation And Management (CREAM) program has always paid off. (Oh look, another acronym).

IDENTITY THEFT

Identity theft is one of the most damaging and costly risks that has unfortunately invaded our lives.

If your identity is stolen, it can cost you:

Your job	*Your credit rating*
Higher insurance rates	*Have loans declined*
Higher credit card fees	*To get arrested*

During the first half of 2005, 46 million Americans records were lost or stolen.

It is estimated that there are currently over 20,000 cases of identity theft each day, representing the fastest growing crime costing 46 to 53 BILLION dollars annually.

The largest purchasers of identity theft information are non-Americans making it almost impossible to catch them.

Recovery from identity theft costs an average of 600 hours and $1,400 for credit repair

Credit repair can take years.

All of your available personal information is now being sold by Data Brokers.

Use the following precautions:

1. ***Do not carry your checkbook or Social Security card in your wallet.*** Make a copy of your Social Security card and black out all but the last four numbers. 30% of identity theft comes from pick pockets. Don't carry identification cards that may use your Social Security Number as an account, member or patient number, such as medical insurance companies.

2. ***Never provide personal information (address, Social Security Number, Drivers License Number, etc.) when not absolutely necessary.*** If anyone asks for information or for completing form or questionnaire, find out if it is required. Often it is not required but desired.

Medical practitioners only need your Social Security Number for a death certificate and for collection of bad credit.

Credit applications only need it for credit review. However, they can use other personal information in lieu of Social Security Number. However, they may not even try and decline credit without it.

3. *Never provide information over the telephone.* You may not be speaking to who you think you are.

4. *Make up 'identifiers'.* Identifiers are personal information 'passwords'. Mother's maiden name, city of birth, name of pet. Make something up. These are not verified by companies, just used as remember-able identifiers.

    For example: Mothers maiden name: Cleopatra
                   City of Birth: Atlantis
                   Pets name: T-Rex

Change passwords every few months or as often as is reasonable.

5. *Require and use unique passwords* for all accounts, online and off-line.

6. *Shred all mail* such as pre-approved applications, con venience loan checks, etc. that might contain personal information or provide access to accounts.

7. *On the Internet, if you receive legitimate looking e-mail from a company asking for information to*

update or verify your account, do not use the included link. Go to the company web address or call them.

8. *Check your credit report regularly* and verify that the activity is only yours. Experian, Equifax and Trans-Union are the three credit bureaus. You can request your own credit report for free. For more information, go to www.FTC.gov/credit.

9. *Use only credit cards and not debit cards for online purchases.* Your maximum responsibility for unauthorized purchases is $50. In addition, get and use a low limit credit card and request that the credit limit not be increased.

10. *If you become a victim,* consider purchasing a guide by Mari J. Frank, *Esquire, From Victim to Victor: A Step by Step Guide for Ending the Nightmare of Identity Theft,* and going to www.idtheftcenter.org on the Internet for help.

Repeating, when you are asked for your Social Security Number, an alarm should go off. Before providing it to anyone, ask two questions:

Is it required that I provide you my Social Security Number? Many times it is **NOT** required.

What happens if I do not provide it? Many times the answer is **"Nothing"**.

If you become a victim of identity theft or would like more information on preventing, in addition to others, there is another book by Mari J. Frank, Esquire, *Safeguard Your Identity.*

UNNECESSARY RISKS

1. *Identify areas of risk.*
2. *Evaluate those risks* and determine if they are necessary or avoidable.
3. *If avoidable, make changes* to eliminate or reduce the risks.
4. *Set up protections if unavoidable.*
5. *Insulate yourself from risks* whenever possible.
6. *Make sure insurance is sufficient* if the risks are unavoidable.
7. *Avoid unnecessary risks.*

THE BOTTOM LINE

Many times we all fail to properly assess our risks until something goes wrong. However, then it is too late to make changes and we must deal with and live with the consequences of those risks. Some time, effort and maybe a little expense may be well rewarded to look at your Unnecessary Risks in advance and take actions to eliminate, avoid and insulate yourself from them to whatever extent you can. At the very least, insure and protect yourself once you identify and understand them.

Bringing It All Together

C H A P T E R   T W E N T Y - S E V E N

Recognizing Success

"I look at what I have not and think myself unhappy;
others look at what I have and think me happy."

— Joseph Roux

WEBSTER'S
"To perceive or acknowledge the validity or reality of."

MINE
"Self aware ability to meet all your needs and most if not
all of your reasonable wants, and probably still have some left over."

One of the sad truths of human nature is that we individually fail to recognize and be satisfied even when we do achieve success. While others will view and recognize our successes, we ourselves may feel discontent, depression and failure. If this happens to you, whatever you do or achieve will only return you disappointment and self perceived failures.

Personal Success is an individual state of mind that will only be achieved when and only when you simply tell yourself that you have achieved it.

King Midas, in his time, was the wealthiest man in the world, yet he died in hunger after killing his daughter.

A recent young entrepreneur sold his software business for $19 million at the ripe old age of 39 but was ashamed to tell his family and peers because he thought it wasn't enough.

Martha Stewart's multi-million dollar personal and corporate empire was brought to its knees after a failure to cover up a few thousand dollars gained in a single stock transaction after giving falsified testimony to authorities.

L. Dennis Kozlowski, multimillionaire Chief of Tyco International charged with securities fraud.

Kenneth Lay & Jeffrey Skilling, formerly of Enron, indicted for fraud.

Andrew Fastow, formerly of Enron, in prison.

Had all these people achieved Personal Success? From the perspective of you, me, everyone else and prior to their downfall, we would have probably said *"Yes"*. So why weren't they content? The simple answer is, *"Because it wasn't enough."*

They saw others that had more and felt that what they had was simply not enough.

Wealth, possessions and conspicuous consumption has become the criterion for recognition and measurement of human pursuits and achievements.

Economics is the study of *"The science that deals with the production, distribution and consumption of commodities"*, which serves for satisfying human needs and desires. If we as humans can never have enough, we can never be satisfied. A paradox.

Laura Nash, senior lecturer in ethics at Harvard Business School, and Howard Stevenson, professor of business administration at Harvard, in their book *"Just Enough: Tools for Creating Success in Your Work and Life"* identify four *"spheres of life"*: Happiness, Achievement, Significance and Legacy. As they have concluded, you should have *"just enough"* in each sphere and not have too much in any one. According to Ms. Nash, *"...it is better to be very good at many important things than to be a superstar at just one."* And more importantly, *"...no amount of success in one area will buy (bring) you satisfaction in the others."*

Ms. Nash provides a simple example that helps put it in perspective.

> *"You're going to enjoy a good cup of coffee a lot more if you don't start worrying about whether it's the best cup you could get."*

People establish unrealistic standards based upon what they see on television and read in the paper. If someone else is making two million dollars, then your measly one million dollar salary just isn't enough.

Each of us has to be able to identify and appreciate our own success and determine how much is enough, both in giving and receiving. To give too much of yourself in pursuing success will doom you to eventual failure.

As Ms. Nash also provides by another example:

> *Mother Theresa felt that attending to her own needs detracted from doing the work of god. She overworked herself to the point of exhaustion and became bedridden thus failing to help others or herself.*

The super achiever may be the best in their one area, however, they will be neglectful in the other three areas: Happiness, Significance and Legacy.

We have all been taught to believe or act as if we believe that:

To have more is better.

Income is a measure for success.

Quality of life is directly related to amount of income.

We deserve more and/or are entitled to better.

We must work more and longer to raise our standard of living.

As Americans, we are entitled to more.

Serving Mammon (riches, greed and possessions) is alright.

The following is condensed from the book *The Wilderness World of John Muir* by Edwin Teale.

In the late 1800's John Muir grew grapes, pears and other fruits. He was the first to ship grapes to Hawaii. An innovator in everything he did, he was financially successful. After ten years and clearing $100,000, he declared to his best friend that he had all the wealth he would ever want. In 1899, the multimillionaire railroad magnate E.H. Harriman financed an expedition to Alaska to seek more riches. When the great wealth of Mr. Harriman was mentioned to Mr. Muir his response was,

"Why, I am richer than Harriman. I have all the money I want and he hasn't."

The moral of the story is: Want what you have, don't want what you don't have, live within your means and know when you have just enough.

I found a story from an unknown source circulating the Internet and have condensed and provided it as another example for recognizing success.

An American with a Harvard MBA was visiting a pier in a small seaside Mexican village when a simple one-person fishing boat docks early one afternoon. As the fisherman unloaded his fish, the American, seeing the quality and size of the fish caught, entered into a conversation with him:

American: *"How long did it take you to catch those fish?"*

Mexican: *"Only a little while."*

American: *"Why did you return so early?"*

Mexican: *"I caught enough for the needs of my family."*

American: *"What do you do with all your extra time then?"*

Mexican: *"I sleep late, fish a little, play with my children, take siesta with my wife, Maria, stroll into the village each evening where I sip wine and play guitar with my amigos. I have a full and busy life."*

American: *"You should spend more time fishing and buy a bigger boat. Then you could buy more boats and build a fleet. Instead of selling to a middle man, you could open your own cannery. You could then expand your distribution, move from this small village to LA or New York City where you could develop more markets."*

Mexican: *"How long would all this take?"*

American: *"15 to 20 years."*

Mexican: *"And then what?"*

American: *"You could sell your business and make millions."*

Mexican: *"Then what would I do?"*

American: *"Then you would retire. You could move back to Mexico, to a small fishing village where you could sleep late, play with your kids, take siesta with your wife and go to the village in the evenings to sip wine and play guitar with your amigos."*

According to William Duby, Editor-in-chief of the American Spirit Newspaper, *"People buy emotionally and then justify it intellectually."* Joe Dominguez's lexicon for Money is, *"That which we spend one-third of our adult lifetimes acquiring, one-third disposing of, one-third recovering from the acquisition and disposal of, and the rest of the time bemoaning the lack of."*

"Which is more important, your honor or your life?
Which is more valuable, your possessions or your person?
Which is more destructive, success or failure?

Because of this, great love extracts a great cost
and true wealth requires greater loss.

Knowing when you have enough avoids dishonor,
and knowing when to stop will keep you from danger
and bring you a long, happy life."
—Lao-Tzu - *"Tao Te Ching"*

Satisfying the insatiable *"More"*.

Joe Dominguez retired after a successful career at the age of 30 by saving *"enough"* from his paycheck to live off the interest for the remainder of his life. He accomplished this by understanding how much is enough and that having more does not satisfy. He created an audio course to help others achieve *"enough"* and donates the entire proceeds of the course to charities.

How often have we all cleaned out our closets, storage rooms, attics, cabinets and garages to give away, throw away or sell for pennies on the dollar the *"stuff"* we worked hard for, spent time and money on to accumulate? Often this is after only minimal usage, if any, of those items.

Next time prior to a purchase, consider three questions. First, does this satisfy a need or a desire or can I live without it? Second, how long must I work to earn the money I will give up in exchange for this item? Third, how much does this represent to the rest of my life?

An example of the third: A purchase of an item for $1,000 represents the $1,000 currently that I must give up for this item which is $60 per year for the rest of my life. (6% return on money otherwise invested). The amount would increase if the interest were left to compound. That might not seem like much, but replace that with $20,000 for the additional cost of a new car wanted but not needed, for example. That would mean $100 per month (or more) that you will be giving up **for the rest of your life**.

Money is merely a paper symbol backed by the Government and pretty much universally accepted as our standard for the exchange of goods and services. It's a means to an end. The accumulation of money does not represent success. What is success is determined by each of us individually for ourselves. Therefore, success is achieved when we personally, and no one else, decide it is. To do so means that we must control money and what it represents instead of it controlling us.

Fulfillment is reaching an end or completion. In other words, realizing when you have just enough.

Give what you need to be satisfied and receive what you need to be fulfilled.

> *Realities are objective.*
> *Perceptions are individual.*
> *Absolutes are universal.*

The management of Enron arranged and recorded business transactions that reported nonexistent income (reality). Their belief was that they had to increase company stock values, increase reported profits and also increase their own compensation to realize success (perception). They defrauded their employees and investors, pursued immoral and unethical business practices, eventually financially ruining the company stock and employee retirement plans, and went to jail (absolute).

The accounting firm auditing Enron did not find or report (if found) the fraud (reality). They believed that the amount they were paid by Enron for their services was to great to risk losing (perception). The accounting firm went out of business upon the financial failure and resulting disclosure of the fraud (absolute).

The reality is that we all have the resources to achieve success.

The perception is to be able to utilize the resources you have and achieve that success instead of focusing on what you don't have or can't achieve.

The absolute is that we all have a limited amount of time to do so.

Make sure your perceptions are aligned with reality because there are always absolutes in the future, positive or negative.

———

A new client, Dr. Bob, made an appointment with me for retirement and income planning. Dr. Bob was a recent retiree in his sixties. We went over his investments and retirement benefits and reviewed his household budget and his want list. I spent some time just talking with him about his practice of medicine.

Dr. Bob had many patients that had died over the years and he said what he remembered most was what a dying person chose to talk about. They would talk about their spouse, their children and grandchildren and the events or times that they missed because of work. They talked about the things they had wanted to do with their lives that they had not, the places they had wanted to go that they had not. Not one had ever said anything like *"I wish that I had spent more time working."*

What was interesting was that Dr. Bob said he was really looking forward to retirement and being able to finally spend time and do things with his children and grandchildren. He had missed much of each of their childhoods during medical school and then with his practice. His wife had passed away a few years ago so he lived alone. As you would guess, his profession as a Doctor had prevented him from spending much of any quality time with his family for many years.

Dr. Bob passed away less than a year after retiring.

RECOGNIZING SUCCESS

1. *Recognize success when you achieve it.*
2. *Know how much is just enough.*
3. *Want what you have.*
4. *Don't want what you don't have.*
5. *Live within your means.*
6. *You must control your money instead of it controlling you.*
7. *Having more does not satisfy.*
8. *Before purchasing, ask yourself:*
   Does this satisfy a need or desire?
   How long must I work in exchange for it?
   How much does this cost the rest of my life?
9. *Give what you need to be satisfied and receive what you need to be fulfilled.*

Realities are objective
Perceptions are individual
Absolutes are universal

THE BOTTOM LINE

Most of us are so blinded by our perceptions and the pursuit of success that we may fail to recognize it when we have achieved it. With achievements, new definitions of success are created. You and you alone must determine what success really is and then the trick is to recognize it. Always distinguish between reality and perception because eventually the absolutes will come.

Know when and what is JUST ENOUGH
or you can never possibly achieve

PERSONAL SUCCESS.

Q. What movie is the following line from?
"Life moves pretty fast.
If you don't stop and look around
once in a while,
you could miss it."

CHAPTER TWENTY-EIGHT

The Secret

"Know where to find the information
and how to use it – that's the secret of success."
— Albert Einstein

WEBSTER'S
"Concealed from general knowledge."

MINE
"That which is known by others, desired and sought by you."

Not knowing The Secret can lead to pitfalls like hate, anger, guilt, jealously, vengeance, self destruction. Feelings of abandonment, betrayal, pain, rejection, inferiority, fear, resentment, tension, bitterness, worthlessness, ineptness, inability, low self esteem. This can result in depression and substance abuse. You may become a victim and/or victimize others.

The Secret is so simple in concept yet so very difficult in application. However, once you learn to apply it, success will no longer be a choice, success will be an absolute.

Are you ready for The Secret? The Secret that is so simple and complex but is given and explained with only one word:

Forgiveness

All too many lives seem to get distracted and derailed simply because of their inability to forgive.

Right now you are either overwhelmed or underwhelmed. But:

Forgiveness releases your inner positive energy.

Forgiveness Restores Balance.

Forgiveness Restores Focus.

Forgiveness Restores Control.

Forgiveness is Self Empowering.

At any given moment, you have available to you a finite amount of time and energy. That time and energy will be utilized, hopefully, in doing something. That something is either positive or negative.

For example, negative time and energy can be spent on:

Hating your spouse for having an affair or at someone for hurting you (physically, emotionally or mentally) or taking something from you.

Being Angry toward your boyfriend/girlfriend for dumping you or your best friend for going out with your boyfriend/girlfriend behind your back. Angry towards a parent that wasn't around during your youth. Angry at a parent, spouse or child for dying or leaving you.

Feeling Guilty about not better supporting or spending more time with your children that live with your ex-spouse. Guilty about having failed or wrongfully hurting someone else. *Guilty* with the belief that you are the cause of your parents divorce.

Being Jealous of what someone else has that you have not.

Wanting to seek Vengeance for something bad or wrong that someone did to you.

Your instinctive response to one of an endless number of examples, is probably, *"How do you expect me to forgive that drunk driver that ran the stop light putting me in the hospital where I almost died?"*

The answer is obvious. You are not forgetting the experience or minimizing or justifying the action, and certainly you are going to try to prevent something bad from ever happening again or being repeated. This is not suggesting you ignore what happened but rather you learn from it, take precautions for any repeat or other wrongdoing, and forgive, yourself and/or others.

In my example, you are first victimized by the drunk driver and then the insurance company and legal system that you thought existed for your protection. You are forgiving them for you, not them.

The question is: How long do you let this incident continue to make you a victim?

Forgiveness is for your benefit, not the other persons.

Dr. Phillip McGraw, Ph.D. Author of the book *Life Strategies: Doing What Works, Doing What Matters* states that *"Forgiveness is about you, not them."*

Dr. Phillip continues, "(Without forgiveness) ... *those who love you don't get you - they get the bitter shell of who you once were."* And, " ... *you either contribute to or contaminate every relationship in your life. If you're dragging the chains of hatred, anger, and resentment* (I would add guilt) *into your other relationships, then, clearly, you are contaminating them."*

Dr. Phil *goes on to state that, "Some of the most tragic lives I have encountered have been those people who allowed hate, anger, and resentment* (don't forget guilt) *to consume them, whereas on the inside, behind the brittle layers of pain and hostility, they were kind and loving."*

In the January 2005 issue of *Harvard Women's Health Watch*, and research by Frederick Luskin Ph.D., director of the Stanford Forgiveness Project, research has established that forgiveness:

Reduces Stress. Stress tenses muscles, elevates blood pressure, increases sweating, causes chronic back pain, headaches and stomach pain. With stress, the body releases chemicals: Cortisol, Adrenaline, Noradrenaline. These chemicals disrupt the bodies immune system causing hypertension leading to coronary artery disease.

Forgiving improves heart rate and blood pressure.

Forgiving brings more happiness making you and no one else responsible for your happiness.

Rebecca was divorced seven years ago after sixteen years of marriage that ended as a result of her husbands infidelity. Now after seven years, she is still angry over the ended relationship with the person that she expected to spend the rest of her life with. Her life consists of poor sleep with frequent crying spells. After taking an audio course from Fredrick Luskin Ph.D., she called her ex-husband telling him that she forgave him. After that, she finally put her life together and her failed relationship behind, happily moving forward.

Debra, a lady in her early fifties, her husband dies of cancer. Three years later she is still angry at him for leaving her and sits alone in her home crying. She is unable to return to work or concentrate on moving forward and putting her life together. Unfortunately, she still is not able to forgive.

"Forgiveness is not about letting anyone off the hook but yourself" according to Dr. Luskin, author of *Forgive for Good.*

"... When individuals were able to forgive, they experienced greater joy and more profound sense of control over life and less depression." According to Charlotte Witvleit, Ph.D., psychology professor at Hope College in Holland, Michigan, based upon results of studies.

---

*"Anger makes you smaller, while forgiveness
forces you to grow beyond what you were."*

— Cherie Carter-Scott

Forgiveness is finding a resolution within yourself for closure so that the action, incident, whatever, is put behind you. Once there is forgiveness, it's over and all your time and energy can be focused forward with positive actions.

With forgiveness, you regain control of your life from those that you would have otherwise permitted to continue to control you, including yourself. For some, forgiving yourself for a wrongdoing towards another can be more difficult than forgiving someone else from a wrongdoing towards you.

---

*With forgiveness, you are empowered
and everyone else is powerless.*

THE BOTTOM LINE

Forgiveness of yourself and of others restores your balance and releases your time and energy for positive pursuits. Forgiveness is a reconciliation of the past and taking your first step forward. Forgiveness is control and empowering to yourself and over all others.

Forgiveness is for your benefit, not the other persons.

Forgiveness *is for your benefit,* not the other persons.

Forgiveness is for your benefit, *not the other persons.*

A. Answer to previous chapter movie line question.

"Life moves pretty fast.

If you don't stop and look around

once in a while, you could miss it."

Ferris Bueller's Day Off

Q. What movie is the following line from?

"Daniel ... for man with no forgiveness in heart,

life worse punishment than death."

CHAPTER   TWENTY-NINE

Taking Action

"Even if you're on the right track, you'll get run over if you just sit there."
— Will Rogers

WEBSTER'S
"The process of doing."

MINE
"The single most important thing that separates the few from the many."

As Dr. Phillip McGraw writes in his book *Life Strategies: Doing What Works, Doing What Matters*, *"Life rewards action. People don't care about your intentions. ... you must commit to measuring yourself and everyone else on the basis of outcomes."*

Robert Stevenson of Seeking Excellence in his book *How to Soar Like An Eagle in a World Full of Turkeys* writes that *"Most people seem to have good intentions, but no follow-through. ... The principles are sound. The methods are proven. The rewards are there. The choice is yours."*

Sun Tzu, in his book *For Success, How to Use The Art of War,* states that *"Inactivity causes more loss of opportunity than mistakes in the choice of methodology."*

Talk is cheap — Actions speak louder than words

I quote the above referenced sources because of their personal knowledge, achievements and accreditations. They have great clarity and elegance and accentuate your choice: *To do or not to do.* (Sorry).

WORDS SAY A LITTLE,
ACTIONS SAY A LOT,
CONTRADICTION SAYS EVEN MORE.

Excuses are many and easy to find. To have the ability and knowledge to do better, to be better, to achieve your own defined Personal Success, and choose not to use it, is more than just sad or shameful. Not only are you letting others that care down, more importantly, you perform a disservice to yourself by letting you down. By not living up to your potential, you resign yourself to living up to your low expectations.

It's not the failures you'll remember or the times you didn't quite make it. It's not the things that didn't work or what you couldn't do. It's not those times you were turned down or looked over.

What will haunt your memories
are the times you didn't even try.

———

The west Florida coast is occasionally cursed with 'Red Tide'. Red Tide results from the explosive growth of a specific alga. This alga is toxic to many types of marine life, and causes death to those species.

A Sand Dollar is a fragile disk which is the skeletal part of a marine animal. It is round, somewhat flat and measures two to four inches in diameter. In the middle of the top of the Sand Dollar are five sets of pores arranged in a petal pattern. When they are still alive and wash up on the beach, they will bleach from a gray to a tan color, and die from exposure to the sun. Sand Dollar's are resistant to the Red Tide.

When Red Tide appears, it kills the natural predator of the Sand Dollar and increases its numbers.

Early one morning after a storm while walking down the beach on Sanibel Island, I watched as a young girl walked towards me picking up Sand Dollars that had washed up onto the beach from the storm. Since there had been some Red Tide offshore and a storm the previous evening, there were a larger number than usual.

One by one she tossed them back into the water as I approached her. Upon reaching her I asked what she was doing. She replied, *"If the Sand Dollars don't get back into the water, they will dry out and die."*

As I turned and looked down the beach in the direction she was walking, I saw hundreds of Sand Dollars that had washed up. I turned back to the young girl and said *"There are so many. How do you expect to make a difference?"* The young girl took a moment in thought while she looked down the beach at the hundreds of Sand Dollars laying there. She stooped to pick one up and tossed it into the water saying, *"I made a difference for that one."*

(Variation of a story with unknown origins)

Be more than just the exception, be exceptional – be successful!

A. Answer to previous chapter question.

"Daniel ... for man with no forgiveness in heart,
life worse punishment than death."

The Karate Kid

CHAPTER THIRTY

The Final Chapter

Is Up To You!

REAL LIFE

My thanks to the many successful people that contributed in creating this book. Some are aware of their contributions, some are not. However, they all have provided me invaluable experiences and lessons and most importantly the privilege in being a part in accomplishing their own individually defined and desired personal success.

BOOKS

(Highlighted books are highly recommended)

Anatomy of an Illness by Norman Cousins

The Art of the Advantage: 36 Strategies to Seize the Competitive Edge by Kaihan Krippendorff

Blink by Malcolm Gladwell

Call of The Mall by Paco Underhill

Creating Your Future: Personal Strategic Planning for Professionals by George L. Morrisey

Flow by Mihaly Csikszentmihalyi

From Victim to Victor, A Step by Step Guide For Ending The Nightmare of Identity Theft by Mari J. Frank, Esquire.

How To Soar Like An Eagle In A World Full Of Turkeys by Robert Stevenson

Human Motivation by David C. McCelland

Just Enough: Tools for Creating Success in Your Work and Life by Laura Nash and Howard Stevenson

Life Strategies: Doing What Works, Doing What Matters
by Phillip C. McGraw, Ph.D.

Masters of Success by Dr. Ivan Misner, Ph.D.

The Money Book For The Young, Fabulous & Broke by Suze Orman

Objection by Nancy Grace

Personal Space by Robert Sommer

Reclaiming My Soul from the Lost and Found, by Lisa Whaley

Safeguard Your Identity by Mari J. Frank, Esquire

Social Foundations of Thought and Action: A Social-Cognitive Theory by Albert Bandura

The 9 Steps To Financial Freedom by Suze Orman

21 Success Secrets of Self Made Millionaires by Brian Tracy (a study program)

Updating Estimates of the Economic Costs of Alcohol Abuse in the United States by H. Howard

The Wilderness World of John Muir by Edwin Teale

Wisdom for a Young CEO by Douglas Barry

Work and Motivation by Victor H. Vroom

STUDIES

University of Washington survey on New Year's resolutions by Elizabeth Miller and Alan Marlatt

Chicago Smell & Taste Treatment and Research Foundation, Study on body odors

California State University, Study on Impressions

NYU Medical Center, Dr. Jonathan Whiteson study of heart attach recovery

University of Texas, study on aging frailty

The Corporate Strategy Board, study on Scenario Planning

Harvard University, study on confidence and goal achievement

Harvard Negotiation Project, Study on Negotiation

University of California at Berkeley and Point of Purchase Institute, Study by J. Jeffrey Inman and Russell s. Winer on purchasing.

ARTICLES

Healthgrades, Patient Safety In American Hospitals, July 2004

Institute of Medicine, To Err is Human: Building a Safer Health System, November 1999

Center for Disease Control, Family History Initiative, Dr. Paul Yoon

Personalized Medicine Research Center, Dr. Cathy McCarty on genomics

University of Cincinnati, Dr. Stephen Liggett, professor of medicine

Classroom goals, structures, and student motivation in the Journal of Educational Psychology 84(3) by C. Ames

Women's Entertainment Television, Women's impressions from Men

Yahoo! Autos:, November 2003

Follow your Passion, Kymberlee Weil of Mixed Grill

Simplicity, Elaine St. James